This book is designed both for the spouse or partner of the anxious person and for the person with anxiety currently engaged in a relationship.

This book provides information regarding the management of life while keeping your fears and insecurities in check. It allows individuals to understand their emotions and see things from a broader perspective. It will also help to improve certain skill set which will enable to manage relationship issues in a much healthier way rather than distancing from your partner and assuming stuff all the time.

Chapter 1: Understanding anxiety

Individuals with generalized anxiety disorder (GAD) are likely to experience disability in various areas of their lives, including relationships with family, friends, and partners. When you live with GAD, you might be vulnerable to marital distress and be at a higher risk of divorce. However, difficulties in your relationships might signify treatment difficulties — those with disabilities in this zone don't get a positive outcome in treatment for the long term.

While you may be very concerned about your family, friends, colleagues, and others, you may be using pessimistic tactics to cope with this worry. This will erode, over time, the very relationships that you work so hard to preserve.

1.1 Anxiety triggers

1. Health issues

A health condition that is bothersome or complicated, such as cancer or a chronic illness, can cause anxiety or make it worse. This form of trigger is very effective due to its immediate and personal feelings.

By being positive and communicating with your doctor, you will help reduce the anxiety caused by health problems. Speaking to a therapist can also be helpful because they may help you learn how to handle your feelings around your diagnosis.

2. Medications

Some over-the-counter medications(OTC) and prescription can cause anxiety symptoms. That's because you may feel uncomfortable or unwell with the active ingredients in these medications. Those feelings can cause a sequence of events in your mind and body that can lead to increased anxiety symptoms.

Medicines that can cause anxiety include:

• birth control pills

• cough and fever medicines

• weight loss medications

Speak to the doctor about how these medications make you feel and look for an alternative that does not activate the anxiety or make your symptoms worse.

3. Caffeine

To wake up, many people rely on their morning cup of joe, but it can potentially cause or exacerbate anxiety. People who display panic disorder and social anxiety disorder are especially prone to the anxiety-inducing effects of caffeine, according to one report.

Act to cut the caffeine intake wherever possible by adding non-caffeinated alternatives.

Here's a range to try on decaffeinated coffee and tea.

4. Skipping meals

Your blood sugar will drop when you don't eat. That can result in jittery hands, and a rumbled tummy. It can cause anxiety too.

It is important to eat healthy meals for several reasons. It gives you strength and essential nutrients. If you can't find time for three meals a day, balanced snacks are a perfect way to reduce low blood sugar, anxious or stressed feelings and anxiety. Notice food may have an effect on your mood.

5. Negative thinking

The mind governs a lot of the body, and with anxiety, that's definitely real. When you're upset or irritated, the words that you're telling yourself can cause greater anxiety.

If you have a knack of using a lot of negative terms when talking about yourself, it's good to learn to refocus your vocabulary and emotions before you begin that route. In this method, working with a therapist can be incredibly beneficial.

6. Financial concerns

Anxiety can be triggered by worries about saving money or having debt. Unforeseen bills or worries about money are causes, too.

Learning how to handle these types of triggers may require professional advice from a financial advisor, for example. Feeling like you have a partner in the process, and a guide will ease your concern.

7. Parties or social events

If it does not sound like fun to be in a room full of strangers, you are not alone. Events that allow you to make small talk or communicate with people you don't know can cause anxious feelings that can be classified as social anxiety disorder.

Whenever possible, you should also bring along a friend to help alleviate your fears or uneasiness. But working with a therapist often is crucial to find coping strategies that make these incidents more manageable in the long run.

8. Conflict

Problems in relationships, disputes, disagreements — these conflicts can all cause anxiety or make it worse. If conflict triggers you in particular, then you might need to learn techniques for conflict resolution. Often, speaking to a therapist or other specialist in mental wellbeing to learn how to handle the emotions that cause such disputes.

9. Stress

Everyday stressors such as traffic jams or missing your train will bring anxiety to everyone. Yet long-term or persistent stress can lead to long-term anxiety and symptoms worsening, as well as other health issues.

Stress can also lead to habits such as missing meals, drinking alcohol, or failing to sleep enough. Such factors may also cause anxiety or exacerbate it.

Treating and avoiding stress also involves developing strategies for dealing with it. A therapist or counselor may help you learn to identify and cope with your sources of stress when they become stressed or troublesome.

10. Public events or performances

A common cause of anxiety is public speaking, speaking in front of your manager, competing in a competition, or even reading aloud. If this is needed by your job or hobbies, your doctor or therapist can work with you to learn ways to feel more relaxed in those settings.

Positive support from friends and colleagues will also make you feel more relaxed and confident.

11. Personal triggers

Such causes can be difficult to recognize, but a specialist in mental wellbeing should be qualified to help you recognize them. This may start with an odor, a spot, or even a song. Specific causes remind you of a poor memory or traumatic experience in your life, whether consciously or unconsciously. Individuals who show post-traumatic stress disorder (PTSD) also experience situational stimuli causing anxiety.

It can take time to recognize personal triggers, but it's vital for you to learn how to resolve them.

1.2 Tips for identifying triggers

Once you can find and recognize the causes, you can learn to prevent and deal with them. You may develop coping mechanisms tailored to tackle stimuli when they arise.

Here are three tips for identifying triggers:

• Start a journal. Note down when the distress is evident, and note what you think might have contributed to the cause. Some applications can also help monitor your anxiety.

• Consult with therapist. It can be difficult to recognize certain causes of anxiety, but a mental health specialist has training that can help. You can find causes by using talk therapy, journaling, or other approaches.

• Be honest with yourself. Anxiety can give rise to negative thinking and poor self-assessments. Due to the nervous responses, this may make it difficult to recognize causes. Be gentle with yourself, and be prepared to discuss issues in your history and find out how they could affect you today.

1.3 Symptoms of anxiety

The most common symptoms of anxiety include:

- uncontrollable worry
- fear
- a fast heartbeat
- difficulty sleeping or insomnia
- difficulty concentrating
- physical discomfort
- muscle tension
- tingling
- restlessness
- feeling on edge
- irritability

You may suffer from an anxiety disorder if you experience these symptoms on a daily basis for six months or longer. There are other types of anxiety disorders, too. Such signs may be different from GAD. You can experience, for example, panic disorder:

- a rapid heartbeat or palpitations
- sweating
- shaking

- trembling
- feeling as if your throat is closing

1.4 How The Critical Inner Voice Damages Relationships

The critical inner speech is the inner voice or pattern of thought that runs in the mental context and sometimes in the foreground. It speaks, criticizes, and judges us and others. Much of the vital inner voice is created in infancy. Children acquire perceptions and opinions from their environments and do not have the cognitive capacity to assess whether they are right. The further negative behaviors that are witnessed and directed towards the child, the more the child develops a negative core thinking.

"Medical studies examining the structure, roles and or sources of the negative thinking mechanism or voice have explained its role in the intergenerational transmission of negative parental attitudes, behaviors, and defenses" Emotionally underdeveloped parents (or caregivers) are likely to project their own insecurities or parts of themselves that they do not like onto their children. Children will not have the opportunity to recognize that the parents have this issue and will adopt any mark they encounter. When you've been branded as evil, bad, not very bright, etc., as your role in the family, you're unconsciously trying to replicate the same role in your interpersonal relationships.

The vital voice inside will promote anything that supports it or condemns anything that contradicts it's beliefs. And it can positively target partners trying to express their affection and promote actions that will cause a partner to react negatively.

"To a large degree, they behave in ways that cause violent, frustrating reactions. For example, partners withhold the affectionate, caring responses that were originally desirable, provoking frustration and rage among themselves with forgetfulness, thoughtlessness, and other forms of direct or indirect hostility. Ultimately, partners are frustrated to the point where they actually find themselves speaking out the voices of the husband/wife in an angry reaction to the provocation." This causes partners to withdraw, create the defenses, and experience a distance from each other that is safe for the critical inner voice.

Attacking

Whenever we want to let down our defenses, get intimate with a partner, and be open, the vital voice inside will surface, picking up on your insecurities. It magnifies out of proportion behavior and insecurities, generating a state of insecurity which can make it difficult for us to be ourselves. Those are the thoughts as if I'm not good enough, and she might consider someone better than me, why did I say I sound like an idiot. For example, in my own personal experience, I sometimes think my inner critical voice would start criticizing my appearance before meeting someone for a date. I once walked through a few shops on the way to a date, and the voice just kept saying things like why I put on this top I look terrible, she will be disappointed when she sees me and doesn't want to see me again, my shape isn't attractive, etc. I even considered not showing up on this specific day, and found myself walking into shop after shop desperately looking for a top that would make me feel better about myself. I ended up buying a top that wasn't really much better than my original top, getting an hour late to that date. As a consequence, I felt stressed on edge and couldn't be myself.

Blaming

The vital voice inside focuses on and magnifies any shortcomings an intimate partner has. It can be voices like he's too insecure, she'll leave me, she'll just string me along, he's too dull and so on. Considering the objective perspective to look at the situation is one way to distinguish between the vital inner voice and a legitimate partner concern. Will a neutral individual from outside look at the situation draws a similar inference. For instance, if a partner regularly flirts with anyone they meet giving compliments, seeking reasons for touching people, it's a fair assumption that they're flirtatious, and that may trigger problems. Yet a partner who doesn't go out too much and instead comes home an hour later than they agreed on one occasion; has actually come home late for a legitimate cause. The vital inner voice is that situation could persuade you that it was due to them cheating on you.

If you're caught up in shallow stuff like she's eating up to fast, I can't stand her shoes, and her boobs aren't big enough, etc., this is most probably the critical inner voice. A particular type of vital voice inside would be most vocal in people with avoiding style of connection. It acts as the ideal distancing device, as they won't want to spend time with a partner if they can't even bear the breathing sound of that partner!

"She started with the thoughts she had initially mentioned, but then went on to show a whole point of view that was dismissive of her and her husband. Her tone was arrogant and derogatory. After giving time to fully articulate those thoughts, I asked her where she felt these thoughts had originated. Whose opinion was this? Asking such questions is the second step in Voice Therapy. She quickly answered that she felt it was her mother's voice talking to her. She revealed that her mother had often shown critical and controlling attitudes toward men. She realized that this incorporated point of view of her mother's was sabotaging her relationship, a relationship that is precious to her."

Withholding

The meaning of withholding in relationships is holding back positive or desired responses from a partner. This means not wanting to show devotion, support, or affection and, therefore, not wanting to receive attention. Thoughts like he's cheating on you, he doesn't really love you, I don't want her to get comfortable why would I do that for her. This can also take a more passive defensive approach, such as being too busy or procrastinating to forget things.

1.5 Taking control of the voice

Recognize - The first step to overcoming the voice is the ability to recognize it as distinct rather than part of you. Avoid and mark it as 'the vital voice is beginning again' as soon as you start hearing the sound. Taking it out from the first person, replace 'I' with 'You,' if this helps, give it a different name like little miss moody. This will help you begin to realize it's just a voice and not the reality.

Challenge –Challenge constantly what the voice tells you, or why it finds it to be false. Think back to where that opinion was created, was it something that your brother mocked you at school, or something that a bully told you. Is it just a totally crazy thought, then say it. When you fail to say positive things to yourself, listen to positive meditations or videos on YouTube for affirmation. When you used to experience disappointment in your youth, it's possible you won't know a lot of different positive reassurances, and it will help you gain some.

Meditation and Therapy -- Meditation helps to maintain control of speech and avoid spiraling thoughts. If you are struggling to gain voice control, then psychotherapy is advised to help you to work through any residual trauma that holds you back.

The Difference Between Healthy and Obsessive Love

In a stable love relationship, the infatuation stage of romantic love typically occurs in the early months. It may include constant love object thoughts and wishing to spend every moment with that person. A stable love relationship typically develops over time such that the near desperate severity and fervor of infatuation is no longer involved. Over the years, healthy love continues to grow to include commitment, intimacy, and a strong regard towards the other person as an individual and their needs. Healthy relationships require both partners to feel valued, cared for, and appreciated and to encourage the autonomy of each person and the enjoyment of their own professional life, social interests, and friendships outside the love relationship.

Unfortunately, obsessive love has been romanticized for decades in literature, as well as in the media, when the media came into being. Though Romeo and Juliet's joint deaths and even several of the new romantic films, becoming fascinated with the object of one's affection is always held up as something to aspire to rather than getting the potentially catastrophic consequences of actions as the films fade into black.

The difference between prosperous and obsessive love is that the feelings of infatuation become intense with the latter, growing to the point that they become obsessions. Obsessive love and jealousy is a sign of mental health issues and is a sign found in approximately 0.1 percent of adults. Individuals suffering from irrational paranoia frequently perceive small events like a coworker saying hello to their spouse or romantic partner, seeing a passerby as clear evidence that their loved one is unfaithful. It has been found that male alcoholics are particularly susceptible to developing irrational jealousy. Females prefer to develop intense love towards people they meet rather than for a stranger. The objects of affection for obsessively loving women are mostly people who have been in the role of aid in their lives. In the few cases where obsessive love causes abuse, both men and women tend to be at similar levels perpetrators of such abuse. Risk factors for the development of obsessive love include a lack of full-time jobs, as well as having family members with psychological issues, particularly a delusional disorder.

1.6 What are the signs of obsessive love?

Obsessive love can be differentiated from a stable romantic relationship by possessing addictive characteristics apart from obsessive envy. The person who suffers from obsessive love, for example, appears to want to spend excessive time with their object of love, so they think intensely about and participate in activities that keep them in contact with their object of love to an intense degree. They may restrict their participation in sporting activities or other social interactions, including being disabled to the point of being unable to function. An individual who loves obsessively can engage in escalating psychological control devices, or other types of control, in an effort to hold his object of love near. Examples of this include monitoring money or food, and stalking or using abuse in extreme cases. The person who is obsessively in love, as well as the object of that love, may, respectively, be dependent upon and co-dependent upon one another. The person who loves obsessively will act as though he was addicted to his object of love. The target of obsessive affection, in effect, may have difficulty setting reasonable limits and constraints on obsessive behaviors.

1.7 What causes obsessive love?

The procedure followed by mental health practitioners to diagnose obsessive love requires assessing the individual to ensure that psychiatric problems that might interfere with this symptom are identified and handled when interfere. Many such diseases include schizophrenia, bipolar disorder, delusional disorder, obsessive-compulsive disorder, personality disorder, or organic brain syndrome (caused by a medical condition). Dangerous signs that someone is suffering from obsessive love can include:

• Low self-esteem / a tendency to seek constant reassurance

• Obsessively thinking about their beloved object

• Making frequent calls, texts and/or faxes to the object of love

• Unnecessary intense attention to the object of love

• A desire to feel excessively good or bad about others (not balanced)

• A tendency to focus on only the good or the negative aspects of their loved one

• Having issues while focusing on work, recreation, socializing, or other parts of their lives outside of the object of their affection

• Attempts to monitor or otherwise control their partner's life and activities

• Indefinite joy, to the point of relief, when having the opportunity to get in touch with or be with the person they love

1.8 How can you overcome the unhealthy love?

Treating unhealthy love often involves psychotherapy for the person suffering and for their love object, especially if the two people are in a relationship at the moment with each other. Counseling may help and can include encouraging all parties to envision their relationship in a healthy way, as well as using affirmations and other strategies to improve their self-confidence. Medication should be used to treat any underlying mental condition, if possible. If the person with obsessive love has begun to manifest threatening or otherwise unsafe behaviors, then legal actions such as involving the police and imposing restraining orders and protective measures may be appropriate.

Chapter 2: Anxiety in a relationship

Many people, at some point, feeling a little uncertain about their relationship, especially in the early stages of dating and making a commitment. It is not uncommon, and you usually don't need to worry about passing doubts or fears, particularly if they don't have too much effect on you.

Yet often these nervous thoughts expand and float into your daily life.

2.1 Symptoms of relationship anxiety

Here's a look at some possible symptoms of relationship anxiety:

Wondering if you matter to your partner

 "The most popular form of relationship anxiety is, 'Do I matter?'. 'Or' are You there for me? '" Explains Robertson. "It refers to a basic desire to communicate, contribute, and feel safe in a relationship." For example, you may be worried that:

• your partner wouldn't miss you a lot if you weren't around

• they may not be offering help or support if anything bad comes up

• they only want to be with you because of what you can do for them.

Having doubts that your partner doesn't have feelings for you

You've exchanged I love you's (or maybe something like I really, really like you). They seem delighted to see you and make kind gestures, such as taking you lunch or going out of their way to see you around.

Yet the nagging question still can not be shaken: "They don't really love me." Perhaps they're slow to react to physical affection. Or they don't answer texts for a few hours — even a day. You wonder if their thoughts have changed when they suddenly seem a little distant.

These feelings can arise from time to time, but if you have concerns about relationships, these thoughts may become a fixation.

Worrying they want to break up

A good relationship will give you a feeling of affection, protection, and happiness. Wanting to hang on to these feelings is completely natural, and hope that nothing will happen to disrupt the relationship.

But often, these thoughts can turn into a constant fear that your partner will abandon you.

When you change your actions to ensure their continuing love, this anxiety may become troublesome.

For example, you might:

• avoid raising concerns, such as constant lateness, that are important to you in a relationship

• neglect when your partner does things that annoy you, such as bringing shoes inside your house

• stress about them getting pissed at you, even though they don't seem upset.

Doubting that it won't last long

If you have relationship anxiety, you can be doubtful of you and your partner's compatibility, even when things are going smooth in the relationship. You may even wonder if you're happy, or if you just think you're happy.

In response, you may begin to concentrate your attention on minor differences — they love country music, but you listen to folk-rock music — and overemphasize the importance of such differences.

Compromising the relationship

Destructive behaviors can arise from relationship anxiety.

Signs of destruction

Examples of things that might hurt a relationship include:

• Having arguments with your partner

• driving them away by pretending that nothing is wrong while you're in pain

• violating relationship limits, such as having lunch with an ex without telling your partner

You might not do such things intentionally, but the underlying objective — whether you know it or not — is typically to decide how much your partner cares.

For starters, you might assume that resisting your attempts to drive them away means they really love you.

Yet picking up on the underlying motive is very difficult for your partner.

Reading into their words and actions.

A tendency to overthink the words and behavior of your partner may also indicate concern about relationships.

They may not want to hold hands. Or, they insist on keeping all their old furniture when you take the plunge and move in together.

Yeah, both of these can be indicators of a possible problem. But they're more likely to have sweaty hands or just enjoy the living room setup.

Missing out on the good times

Still not sure whether you struggle with anxiety around relationships?

Take a step back and ask yourself: "Do I Spend more time thinking about this relationship than enjoying the relationship? "May this be the case during difficult periods. Yet if you feel this way more frequently than not, you will probably be struggling with some anxiety about relationships.

2.2 What causes it?

It can take time to understand what's behind your anxiety and committed self-exploration because there's not a single straightforward trigger. You may even find it hard to recognize possible triggers by yourself.

You may not know a reason for the anxiety. But no matter what you make of it, the underlying causes usually represent a desire for connection. There are some common factors that can play a role:

Previous relationship experiences

reminders of events that have happened in the past that tend to influence you, even though you think you've gotten over them completely.

You may be more likely to experience relationship anxiety when a former spouse: • deceived you

• left you suddenly

• lied about their feelings for you

• manipulated you about the essence of your relationship

It's not uncommon to have difficulty putting faith in anyone again after you've been hurt — even though your current partner shows no signs of coercion or dishonesty at all.

Any causes, whether or not you are aware of them, can still remind you of the past and cause fears and insecurities.

Low self-esteem

Often a low self-esteem may lead to insecurity and anxiety in the relationship.

Some older research shows that when experiencing self-doubt, people with lower self-esteem are more likely to doubt the feelings of their partners. This can happen as a projection form.

In other words, feeling disappointed in yourself will make it easier for you to believe that you are perceived the same way by your partner.

In comparison, people with higher levels of self-esteem appeared to support themselves when experiencing self-doubt through their relationship.

Attachment style

The attachment style that you develop in childhood can have a significant effect on our adult relationships.

If your parent or caregiver addressed your needs immediately and provided love and support, you've probably formed a stable attachment style.

When they have not regularly met your needs or encouraged you to grow independently, your attachment style will be less stable.

Insecure attachment styles can contribute to anxiety about relationships in a number of ways:

• Avoiding attachment may lead to anxiety about the degree of commitment you make or deepen intimacy.

• On the other hand, a nervous attachment can also lead to worries that your partner may abandon you suddenly.

Keep in mind that having an unstable style of attachment does not mean that you are destined to always feel anxiety about relationships.

"As you can't shift your relationship style from one kind of personality to another, so you can't change it absolutely," says Jason Wheeler, Ph.D. "But you should definitely make enough adjustments that an unstable style of attachment will not hold you back in life."

A tendency to question

An insecurity for relationships can also be factored by a questioning disposition.

You may need to ask yourself about all potential situational outcomes before you settle on a course. Perhaps may you're just getting used to carefully consider every decision.

If you want to ask yourself more questions about your decisions, even after you've made them, you'll probably spend some time still questioning your relationship. It isn't always a problem. In reality, taking time to think about choices you make, particularly important ones (like romantic engagement), is typically safe.

If you find yourself repeating the same cycle of questioning and self-doubt that doesn't go productive anywhere, it might become a problem, though.

2.3 Effects of anxiety on relationships

There's a lot of knowledge about how anxiety impacts our health — mentally, emotionally, and physically. Did you consider the potential effect anxiety has on your relationship's health?

Anxiety may trigger periods of panic, fear or overwhelming feelings, and a general sense of unease and stress. It can take over your thoughts and make other parts of your life bleed.

If you sense a strain on your relationship, anxiety can have a part to play. Could your anxiety (or your partner's) put your relationship in danger?

Here's how and why relationships are ruined by anxiety and what you can do to stop it.

Anxiety breaks down trust and connection.

Anxiety triggers concern or worry, which is a given moment that may make you less aware of your true needs. This can also make you less attuned to your partner's needs. If you're concerned about what could happen, it's hard to pay attention to what's going on. When you're frustrated, your partner can feel like you're not there.

This way, train the brain to live in the moment. Take a break and focus on what you know (as opposed to what you don't know) if you encounter a fear or anxiety that causes your mind to wander from the truth or the present moment. Calm down before taking any action. You should take purposeful measures to create trust within your partner. Share freely when you feel nervous, and deliberately reach out (physically or verbally) to your partner when you would usually withdraw or strike in fear.

Anxiety crushes your true voice, creating panic or procrastination

Someone who appears to be nervous may have difficulty voicing their true feelings. It might also be hard to maintain fair boundaries when asking for the attention or space needed.

Because experiencing anxiety is stressful, you can subconsciously attempt to delay the experience. On the other hand, anxiety may lead you to feel that something needs to be talked about immediately when a brief break can actually be beneficial.

If you're not voicing what you really feel or need, then anxiety becomes greater. However, if you hold them in, your emotions can inevitably spiral off balance. You could get frustrated and defensive.

So let your feelings be known sooner rather than later. A sensation of fear need not be a tragedy for it to be tackled. Approach your partner with empathy, so you are neither panicking nor procrastinating. Find time, too, to unpack some of the thoughts or worries that linger in your mind; they rob your time and energy.

Anxiety causes you to behave selfishly

Since anxiety is an overactive reaction to fear, often someone who experiences it can concentrate too much on their own worries or problems.

Your concerns and fears can bring undue pressure to bear on your relationship. You may feel you need to think about protecting yourself in your relationship, but maybe it will prevent you from being caring and open to your partner.

When your partner has anxiety, you can also build up anger and respond in selfish ways. The behaviors we have and the experiences are infectious. It is especially difficult to keep the stress levels under control when the partner is feeling nervous, frustrated, or defensive.

Please take care of your needs and not your fears. Take a moment to consider the love you have for yourself and your family when you see yourself being afraid or defensive. Demand specifically the support you need to feel loved and understood. Excuse yourself for letting fear get you self-absorbed.

Anxiety is the opposite of acceptance.

A healthy type of concern will warn you that "something is wrong;" it comes from a fast pull to your heart or a tight feeling in your stomach. This signal encourages you to behave, especially when you speak up for someone who is being unfairly handled.

Unhealthy anxiety levels make you feel like an emotional "tar" is almost continuously in your stomach. Anxiety causes you to ignore non-hazardous issues and avoid things that could help you. This can also discourage you from taking positive steps to improve things that affect you in your life because it makes you feel helpless or trapped.

Practice to face uncomfortable situations. You don't have to dismiss an awkward idea or obsess over an uncomfortable situation. If you can, then take positive action. Your partner sometimes only wants you to be present with his or her emotions, and sometimes you need to give yourself the same gift. Through gentle eyes or a soft touch, you can show your presence to your partner, and be present with a calming breath.

Anxiety robs you of joy

Experiencing happiness calls for a sense of protection or independence. Anxiety makes us feel either terrified or constrained. A brain and body conditioned to stress will also have a much harder time enjoying intimacy and sex. Negative thoughts and worries have an effect on the willingness of a person to be present within a relationship and potentially suck the happiness out of a moment.

Don't take yourself too seriously. To combat fear, you can use your sense of humor. Try to have your partner laugh and play. Joy strengthens and comforts the brain emotionally in ways that are essential to a healthy relationship.

As Anxiety Weakens, Your Relationship Strengthens. Building confidence will reduce the power of anxiety within your relationship. Through understanding how anxiety affects your relationships, you will bring about positive change within a complex relationship.

2.4 Steps to get rid of Your Critical Inner Voice

To question our fear, we need to get to know our vital voice inside first. We will try to capture it every time that it comes into our minds. It can be simple at times.

We get ready for a date, and it yells, "You look awful! You're just too fat. Just cover up yourself. He's never going to be drawn to you. "Other times, it's going to be sneakier, even relaxing," just keep it to yourself. Don't compromise or show her how you feel, and you won't get hurt. "This makes us, this voice can also turn on our partner," You can't trust him. The first step to questioning this vital voice inside is to recognize it.

As we continue to raise consciousness and question these divisive attitudes towards ourselves, we also need to make an effort to take action that goes against the guidelines of our vital voice inside. This means, in terms of a friendship, not acting out on the basis of unwarranted insecurities or behaving in any manner that we do not respect. Below are some helpful steps to take:

knowing what you are being told by your Vital Inner Voice. Individuals must first become conscious of what their vital inner voice is telling them to counter their negative attacks. By defining an aspect of their lives where they are especially critical of themselves, they can do this and then pay attention to what the critiques are. As a person learns what the self-attacks are, it's worth articulating them as statements of

44

"you" in the second person. For example, instead of saying, "I feel so lazy and useless," a person might say, "You are so lazy. You're useless." When people use this technique in voice therapy, they're allowed to convey their critical thoughts when they hear or encounter them, and that sometimes leads to them experiencing the frustration that underlies that self-attacking method.

Recognizing from whence the voices come. They also feel profoundly when people verbalize their sensitive inner voices in this way and have insight into the root of their voice-attacks. They have remarkable insight as they begin to realize that their voice attacks' content and tone are old and familiar; their voices convey attitudes toward them as infants.

Often they would say things like, "That's what my father used to say," or "That's the feeling I got from my mother," or "That's the environment in my house." Knowing where their words come from helps people build compassion.

Responding to Your Vital Inner Voice. In the third phase of speech therapy, a person responds to speech attacks again. Those who have thoughts like, "You're so stupid. No one wants to know what you're thinking.

Just sit back in the background and keep your mouth shut!" may reply with statements like, "I'm not stupid! What I have to say is important and worthwhile. A lot of people are interested in me and care about what I think." They might say something like, "The world isn't a place where everyone else is clever, and I'm the only stupid person. I'm no longer in high school; nobody judges us. The truth is people aren't all that smart, and I'm not stupid. We're basically the same: intelligent people who have interesting things to say about what they're thinking and experiencing."

Understanding How Your Voices Influence Your Behavior. People are obviously interested and willing to learn how these habits of self-defeating feelings have affected their experience and affect their present-day actions after voicing and listening to their voices. For example, the person with the voice that he or she is dumb might remember occasions when, as a result of having heard the self-attack, he or she has behaved less able or confident. If people try to alter particular self-limiting habits, gaining an awareness of how the vital inner voice has influenced their behavior is beneficial.

Changing the habits of self-limitation. When people have recognized the ways they are restricting themselves, they will start improving. They will do so by taking two actions: not engaging in the self-destructive conduct that the vital inner voice promotes and the constructive habits that go against the voice's recommendations. A person who is shy, for example, should stop avoiding social interactions and can make a point of engaging in conversations with people.

Odd as it can sound, it can be harder to recognize and address crucial voices inside. Anxiety comes with transition, and getting rid of a criticism inside is no exception. Sometimes, when people start resisting their negative attacks and acting against their orders, the attacks become more frequent and stronger. There are people who have become accustomed to their negative feelings, and they are happy "living with" them, although uncomfortable. Even one woman identified them as sustaining her company. She said when she started getting as many self-attacks, she felt sad and afraid to be without them. Many people falsely believe their vital inner voices are what holds them in line, so they fear they will behave badly if they don't heed them. The more people behave against their vital inner voice, however, the less its impact is on their lives. When they stick it out and follow the voice therapy steps, people become more self-reliant and are able to achieve goals and live free from perceived limitations.

2.5 How to deal with anxiety over relationships

Maintain your freedom. Holding a sense of ourselves apart from our partner is important. The goal for a partnership, as Dr. Seigel said, should be to make a fruit salad and not a smoothie. In other words, we shouldn't forget the important parts of who we are to merge into a couple. Instead, every one of us will strive to preserve the distinctive facets of ourselves that first drew us to each other, even as we step closer. Each of us should stay strong in this way, recognizing that we are a whole person in and of ourselves.

No matter how nervous you are, don't act out. That's easier said than done, of course, but we all know that our insecurities can precipitate some pretty damaging actions. Possessive acts of jealousy will hurt our partner and ourselves in the process. Snooping through their text messages, checking every few minutes by calling them, and getting angry every time they look at another attractive person are all acts we can stop no matter how nervous they make us, and in the end, we can feel much better and more comfortable. What is more important, we will be trustworthy.

Since we can only adjust our half of the relationship, it's always worth talking about whether there are any acts we take that drive us away from our partner. If we behave in a way that we appreciate and yet don't feel like we get what we deserve, we can make a deliberate decision to speak to our partner about it or improve the situation, but we never have to feel betrayed or encourage ourselves to act in ways that we don't appreciate.

Stop looking for warmth. Running to our partner to comfort us when we feel vulnerable leads only to greater vulnerability. Know, these habits come from inside us, and it doesn't matter how smart, sexy, worthy, or desirable our partner tells us we're until we can conquer them inside ourselves. We must aspire to feel good inside ourselves, no matter what, which means embracing the love and affection which our partner directs towards us, truly and fully. But this doesn't mean looking to our partner for reassurance at every step to show we're all right, a pressure that falls on our partner and detracts from ourselves.

In terms of maturity and sharing of kindness, a partnership should be equal. We should clearly express what we want if things sound wrong, but we should not expect our partner to know everything and how to act all the time. When we get into the blame trap, it's a difficult loop to break free from.

Be true to your own self. We all have anxiety, but by being true to ourselves, we will increase our tolerance for the many ambiguities that each relationship eventually poses. We can invest in an individual even if we know that they have the power to do us harm. Having one foot out of the door just holds the relationship as close as it can, and can weaken it entirely. When we allow ourselves to be cherished and feel loved, then we are bound to feel insecure as well, but sticking it out has more benefits than we can imagine. If we take a gamble without making our insecurities influence our actions, the best-case scenario is that the relationship is blossoming, and the worst case is that we are developing inside ourselves. There is no waste of time that has taught us much about ourselves or helped nourish our capacity to love and be vulnerable.

Chapter 3: Managing anxiety

Insecurities: A few of us do have. These are the repetitive feelings that individuals have about the errors they might have made, the shortcomings they might have, and the derogatory views that others might hold towards them. Insecurities can continue frustratingly, and they can always mess with near relations ("You stared at the girl, I saw you looking!"). Expecting people to completely disregard such insecurities isn't possible. Then the problem becomes: What is the healthiest approach to cope with such nagging emotions and thoughts?

3.1 Tell your partner what triggers you

A fairly simple answer might be to express your insecurities to someone you're near to — like a relative or a sexual partner — so that this person might make you feel better. Nevertheless, recent analysis has demonstrated a way that this strategy can often struggle to succeed, and can sometimes backfire. Fundamentally, exposing vulnerability to certain people has the ability to create a whole new form of vulnerability: the fear that other people view you as an insecure person. Say I'm concerned, for example, that I gave a dull lecture for my relationship class and so I want to confess this to my good friend and fellow relationship researcher. Being the sensitive friend she is, Jenny will obviously react by saying things that are comforting ("You rocked that lecture!").

Then after doing that a lot of days, I might start saying, "Huh, lately, I've been feeling pretty awkward about Jenny. She undoubtedly assumes I'm an emotionally unstable adult who badly wants validation and can't take feedback or disapproval. "Unfortunately, from there on, such doubts would make me question any positive word Jenny tells me. I'll figure she's always riding around me on eggshells, seeking to protect my pride and not showing me what she's actually thinking. The positive remarks are less apt to help me feel confident for myself, so I'm going to dismiss them as insincere. And, paradoxically, telling my friend I feel uncomfortable has only exacerbated the issue.

3.2 Passive-Aggressiveness in expressing insecurities

Dr. Edward Lemay and Dr. Margaret Clark presented an innovative blueprint for how this tragic event is progressing. Firstly, the researchers propose that an individual does not need to communicate their insecurities explicitly in order to set the process in motion. There are lots of indirect forms in which people communicate that they feel insecure. For, e.g., imagine my partner makes an innocent remark about his work colleague making a brilliant presentation right around the moment I'm beating myself up about my dull lecture. Just by acknowledging explicitly that this remark made me feel worse for myself, I should have been likely to lash back otherwise. I might end up insulting my partner, storming off in a huff, sulking in my office, or feeling detached or annoyed in general.

When I got a handle on my vulnerability at a later stage, I will possibly look back in shame on this conduct, knowing that my response to my partner was out of context and unjust. It is at this stage where I will start to worry: How did my actions influence the understanding of me by my partner in this instance?

("She may assume he's always going to have to control what She's doing around me ...") And then, while I never consciously confessed to my partner that I felt vulnerable, the process of anxiety will still begin.

Like Other Insecurities, These "Meta" Insecurities Can Be Totally Inaccurate

The analysts further suggest that such assumptions regarding the beliefs of certain individuals are likely to be somewhat off-base. Research suggests that we prefer to assume that other individuals give greater heed to our own actions and feelings than they really do. It's a typical lack in perspective-taking: we presume that something truly makes sense to us at the moment is always what makes a difference to others, so we neglect the likelihood that other individuals concentrate on other issues entirely.

And when I'm off sulking about the lesson, I might hope my partner is well conscious about my ideas and how I feel about them. In the meantime, She may not have really understood my response to her remark, and may rather be curious whether her work colleague got the message regarding the meeting tomorrow. In this situation, any doubts I have regarding my partner's views of me are entirely baseless, as She is not examining my actions at all, let alone experiencing my conduct in a derogatory way.

Moreover, even though our social blunders are observed by certain individuals, they seem not to influence the perceptions of certain individuals towards us about as often as we believe they do. And though my partner realizes that I'm in a poor mood, She'd actually assume that I'm just having a rough day, rather than inferring that I'm a constantly anxious individual. And, though I'm left with this unpleasant meta-perception (I believe my wife perceives I'm an awkward person), the meta-perception is possibly incorrect.

Even Secure People Have Insecurities

Furthermore, the researchers say this phenomenon of vulnerability will happen to everyone. Even if you are normally a safe individual, the fleeting feeling of vulnerability may cause this sequence of events. By voicing your insecurities to a good friend or a potential partner, you might eventually fear that this person may think of you as an unreliable person, which could then cause you to question the positive stuff they tell you.

How Do We Know All This? The Science

The investigators evaluated this pattern in six experiments. They found good support for any aspect of the model overall. For starters, the researchers of one study asked participants to talk of someone special to them — either a significant relationship or a good friend. Participants measured how much they communicated insecurity to this individual (e.g., "I sometimes question this individual if he/she really thinks about me;" "I have often conveyed feelings of pain or rage against that person"), as well as how often they felt this person regarded them as weak (e.g., "This person sees me as fragile and easily harmed"). Finally, participants assessed how often they questioned the sincerity of the positive words and reassurances of their spouse (e.g., "This person censors his / her thoughts and emotions so as not to harm my emotions;" this person sometimes does something he/she doesn't intend to in order to make me feel good). Studies found that while respondents thought they displayed a lot of fear towards their spouse, they often appeared to feel that their spouse perceived them as weak and unstable, which in effect caused them to question the sincerity of their partner.

57

Participants also assessed in another survey how often they questioned the sincerity of the reassurances of their spouse (e.g., "This individual always says something he/she doesn't mean to in order to make me feel good"), as well as how negatively they felt their partners regarded them (e.g., "This person feels I have a range of serious flaws"). The further the participants thought their partners were "walking on eggshells" around them, the more they felt dismissed by their partners.

Most impressively, the researchers performed a quantitative analysis of dyads (people's pairs) to see what happens to the expectations of individuals over time, to see if they compare to fact. In this analysis, the steps mentioned above were performed by 38 dyads — mostly pairs of platonic mates, though also a few intimate couples — twice, five months apart.

For, e.g., if Jenny and I were interested in this research, I would rank how much weaknesses I convey to Jenny, how much I believe Jenny views me as an incompetent individual, and how much I question the sincerity of Jenny when she says me nice stuff. I will also score my caring and concern for Jenny and expectations about how much Jenny cares for me, and Jenny will perform the same metrics about me. Instead, five months on, a second time, we both will be undertaking these exact steps.

By surveying all participants of each group, the researchers were able to determine how realistic impressions of others were really on how their peers or spouses perceived them. In fact, the researchers were best able to investigate causal trajectory by surveying any pair of individuals twice over a five-month period: Which contributes to improvements in what? The researchers once again found good evidence for their model: people who showed more insecurity to their friend/partner appeared to think that this individual viewed them as vulnerable, which in turn led them to question the sincerity of this individual, which in turn led them to assume that this person viewed them more negatively.

With time, this assumption that the individual regarded them more poorly caused the individual to show yet further flaws, and therefore the whole process will begin to escalate with time. Moreover, these impacts existed regardless of the opinions of the mates or spouses. According to these results, if I express my insecurities to Jenny, I will probably subsequently believe that Jenny feels that I am insecure regardless of her actual perceptions of me. Likewise, my belief that Jenny perceives me as insecure will lead me to doubt the authenticity of Jenny, no matter how authentic she is, in fact. And these effects emerged above and beyond self-esteem in all of the studies, suggesting that all of this occurs relatively independently of chronic insecurities.

Conflict Resolution Skills for Healthy Relationships

Conflict is a routine feature of nearly all ties. It may be an effective cause of tension, too. Hence it is necessary to find a settlement for most disputes. That sounds like a simple assumption, but often people are hiding their frustration or only 'getting along to get along.' Others believe they are causing one by resolving a problem, and just stay silent while angry. This is, unfortunately, not a sustainable long-term approach.

Unresolved tension in the partnership will contribute to frustration and more unresolved dispute. Most significantly, continuing tension will potentially have a detrimental effect on your wellbeing and survival.

Sadly even dispute management can be difficult. Improperly managed, efforts at dispute resolution will potentially escalate the confrontation. Researcher John Gottman and his team, for example, researched how people compete, and can accurately determine which spouses will move on to divorce by studying their conflict management skills — or failing in them. (Tip: People that continually question the behavior of their spouse or break down in disputes rather than proactively and politely moving through tension should lookout.) For all who were not born into a household where ideal dispute management techniques were practiced on a regular basis (and — let's face it — how many of us were?), here are several suggestions for managing disagreements.

3.3 Get in Touch With Your Feelings

Only you are interested in an important component of conflict resolution — knowing how you feel and why you feel so.

Your feelings may seem clear to you already, but this isn't always the case. You feel angry or resentful at times but don't know why. Other times, you feel the other person doesn't do what they 'should' do, but you don't know exactly what you want from them, or if it's even sensible.

Using a journal can be an effective way to get in touch with your own feelings, thoughts, and expectations so you can communicate them to the other person better. Often this activity brings up some pretty heavy problems, and psychotherapy can be helpful.

Hone Your Listening Skills

How well we communicate is at least as critical when it comes to successful dispute solving as how well we articulate ourselves. This is crucial to consider the viewpoint of the other party rather than only our own if we want to come to a consensus. In reality, actually making the other party feel noticed and appreciated will also go a long way towards a dispute settlement. Effective communication often allows you to close the distance between the two, and realize where the difference is, etc. Sadly, good communication is an ability that not everybody understands, so it's normal for people to believe they're listening, when in their minds they're just formulating their next response, worrying and telling themselves how the other person is wrong or doing stuff other than trying to understand the other person's viewpoint. It's also common in your own perspective to be so defensive and entrenched that you cannot see beyond your perspective.

Good communication skills are important for good connections. If you're improving a partnership, settling a dispute, or giving help to a experiencing a crisis, strong communication skills may be a lifeline to stability. Know how to be a genuinely compassionate listener, and you will find yourself supported by those who are willing to do the same.

Here's How

1. **Listen, Listen, Listen.** Ask your friend what's wrong, and listen carefully to the comment. Let them sprinkle their fears, frustrations, and other important feelings, keeping eye contact and showing you're interested in what they're saying. Resist the urge to provide unsolicited advice, and simply let them get it out.

2. **Reframe What You Hear.** Summarize and repeat your understanding of what they're saying so that they know you're listening to them and focus on the emotions they may feel. For example, if your friend mentions family concerns, you could catch yourself

thinking, "It looks like things get pretty violent. You sound as though you are hurt. '

3. **Ask About Feelings.** Tell them to further elaborate on what they believe and why. Asking for their emotions offers a strong mental outlet, which could be more beneficial than just relying on their situation's reality.

4. **Keep the Focus on Them.** Instead of delving through your own relevant narrative, hold the attention on them until they feel stronger. When you get the attention back on them easily, you will explain everything that happened to you. They will love the concentrated attention, and they will feel truly cared about and appreciated by this.

5. **Help Brainstorm.** Instead of giving advice at the start, which closes off further discussion of emotions and other interactions, wait until they get their feelings out and then provide them with creative ideas. When you're helping them come up with solutions to work with the pros and cons of everything, they'll actually end up with a plan they feel comfortable with. Maybe after only being able to speak and feel understood, they may feel stronger.

Tips

1. **Stay Present.** Often people are pretending to listen, but they're actually really waiting for their partner to finish talking so that they can utter something they've been secretly rehearsing before pretending to hear. Typically people can feel this, and it's not feeling good. They always seem to lose out on what is being discussed because they are not concentrating.

2. **Don't Give Advice.** I've already discussed this a couple of times, but it's relevant because unsolicited advice will generate tension. It's normal to want to give advice right away to 'fix' the issue with your mate. Don't, Unless expressly asked. While you're trying to help, perhaps what's going to work for you isn't effective for your friend; suggestions might also sound condescending. Unless they inquire for guidance specifically, your partner would generally only want to be noticed and acknowledged, and then seek his or her own ideas.

3. **Trust the Process.** Before plunging into solutions, listening to feelings maybe a little scary, and hearing your friend talk about upset feelings may even make you feel helpless. But by offering support and sitting

in an uncomfortable place with your friend is the most helpful thing you can do, and the solutions can begin to come once the feelings are cleared.

4. **Let Things Even out Over Time.** With all this emphasis on the issues of your mate, it would be hard not to concentrate on your own fair period. Relax in the knowledge that your friend will probably be a better listener to you when you need a friend. If you're doing all the sharing regularly, you should reassess the relationship dynamics. Yet being a successful listener will make you a happier, more compassionate individual and give your interactions a more loving perspective.

How to Practice Active Listening

Effective listening applies to a communication style, which holds you involved in a constructive way with your talking partner. It is the act of listening closely as someone else talks, paraphrasing and thinking back on what's been said, and avoiding judgment and advice. You help the other individual feel understood and respected while you practice active listening. In this sense, the reason for every effective dialog is active listening.

3.4 What Are the Features of Active Listening?

There's more to active listening than simply watching others talk. Once you exercise active listening, you concentrate entirely on what is being said. You listen with all your senses and give the individual speaking your full attention.

Below are some features of active listening:

- Neutral and nonjudgmental
- Patient (periods of silence are not "filled")
- Asking questions
- Verbal and nonverbal feedback to display signs of listening (e.g., smiling, eye contact, leaning in, mirroring)
- Reflecting back what is said
- Asking for clarification
- Summarizing

In this sense, the opposite of passive hearing is active listening.

You get completely involved and immersed in what the other individual is thinking as you listen actively.

You are supposed to act as a sounding board instead of stepping in with your own thoughts and feelings on what's been discussed, almost like a therapist listening to a patient.

The Purpose of Active Listening

Effective communication has the function of gaining other people's trust and helping you appreciate their circumstances. Effective listening requires having a need to hear, as well as giving the speaker encouragement and empathy. It's distinct from crucial listening because you don't analyze the other person's voice with the goal of giving your own view. Rather, the goal is clearly to understand the other party, and maybe to solve their own problems.

Active listening means identifying and removing bad listening habits, such as:

• Becoming lost in your own brain

• Not having reverence for the speaker

• Just hearing shallow context (not understanding real significance)

• Interrupting • Not maintaining eye contact

• Stopping the speaker

• Being distracted • "Topping " the tale (saying "that reminds me of the time ...")

• Ignoring what was discussed in the past

• Asking about details which do not matter

• Focusing too much on little things and missing the big picture

• Skipping what you don't understand

• Daydreaming • Only pretending to pay attention.

Benefits of Active Listening

Relationships

Active listening has many benefits. It helps you to consider another person's point of view and to react empathically. It even lets you ask questions to ensure that you grasp what's being said. Eventually, it validates the speaker and helps them continue to talk longer. It is not impossible to understand how partnerships can profit from this form of listening.

Being a good listener in a partnership requires understanding that the talk is about your partner rather than you. It is especially relevant when a person becomes upset regarding a partnership.

A useful quality is the willingness to consciously respond to a partner who is going through a tough period. However, active listening benefits partnerships because you become not inclined to step in for a "fast answer" while the other party really needs to be understood.

Work

Particularly relevant while you are in a supervisory role or have to communicate with subordinates is good communication at work. Active communication helps you to consider challenges and work together to come up with ideas. This also represents your endurance, which is important at every position of employment.

Social Situations

In social settings, you will benefit from constructive communication when meeting new people. Leading concerns, finding guidance, and learning the expression of the body are all opportunities to know more about everyone you encounter. The other party is more able to speak to you for a longer time while you listen fully. That makes active listening to one of the best ways to make friends out of acquaintances.

Practice Active listening

Focus on these key points to improve active listening:

• Maintain eye contact while communicating with the other person. In general, when you're listening, you can look for eye contact about 60-70 percent of the time. Turn toward the side, and sometimes raise your head. Should not fold your arms, because this means you are not listening to the person.

• Rather than giving unsolicited suggestions or ideas, just paraphrase what was said. You could start by saying, "that is, what you're suggesting ..."

• Should not disturb when anyone else speaks. Should not plan the answers when the other person is speaking; the last thing he or she says can alter the sense of what has been said before.

• Observe nonverbal gestures to pick up on secret context, in addition to listening to what's said. Often facial gestures, tone of voice, and other actions may show you more than just words.

• Shut down the subconscious conversation, as you listen. Avoid a daydream. Around the same moment, it's hard to listen attentively to someone else and to your own inner speech.

• Demonstrate curiosity by posing questions that make clear what's being discussed. Ask questions strikingly transparent to inspire the speaker. Ignore closed yes or no questions which appear to close the discussion.

• Avoid shifting the topic abruptly; it may seem you haven't listened to the other person.

• Be transparent, impartial, and avoid judgment and prejudices while listening.

• Be patient while listening. We can hear even quicker than others can talk.

• Train to earn active listening skills. Watch news interviews to see if the host is actually listening. Know from certain errors.

Example of Active Listening

Below is an example of active listening.

Jessica: I'm sorry to have this dumped on you, but I had a fight with my sister, and we haven't been talking since. I'm upset and don't know with whom to speak.

Karen: No issue. Explain to me details about what happened?

Jessica: Yeah, we've been debating about what to do for the anniversary of our parents. I am still too angry.

Karen: Oh, that is rough. You ought to feel angry that you don't talk because of that.

Jessica: Yeah, she's always making me feel so mad. She hypothesized that I would help her plan this elaborate party — I have no time! In my viewpoint, it's like she couldn't see anything at all.

Karen: Yeah, that is pretty rough. How'd that make you feel?

Jessica: Angry. Furious. Maybe a little guilty that she had all those ambitions, and I was the one to hold them back. I asked her, actually, to do it without me. But this, too, is not right.

Karen: Looks uncomfortable. I think you need some time to figure out how you're feeling.

Jessica: Well, I reckon I do.

History of active listening

In a study conducted in 2011, it was shown that active listening was basically associated with verbal social skills instead of nonverbal skills, suggested that being a good active listener involves effective conversational partners instead of the ability to regulate nonverbal and emotional communication.

What does living with social anxiety means?

Being an active and empathic listener means you are good at initiating and maintaining conversations.

If you strengthen your active listening abilities, you can boost your conversational ability—yet don't anticipate it to significantly alleviate the distress symptoms you currently encounter. For your strong communication abilities to come through, you may need to tackle your distress individually, by counseling or some type of care.

What If Someone Isn't Actively Listening?

What if you're the one talker and the other one isn't a good listener? Most of us have been in such a position where we were annoyed or disinterested by the individual listening. Here are a few suggestions for assisting with this case.

• Choose a subject you both are involved in. This fits especially well when you seek to get to know each other through small talk.

• Develop your own strong communication abilities. Instead of having to speak to someone who really isn't a decent listener, make yourself the interviewer. You may help the individual learn how to become a better listener in doing so.

• Leave the discussion as it becomes obvious that the other party is involved solely in hearing himself talk.

3.5 Practice Assertive Communication

Furthermore, openly expressing your thoughts and desires is a vital part of dispute resolution. Because you already know, saying the wrong thing may be like pouring gasoline on a fire and escalating a confrontation. The thing to keep in mind is to be clear and assertive in saying what's in your mind, without being aggressive or putting the other person on the back foot.

One successful conflict resolution technique is to use 'I ' phrases to place things in terms of how you behave rather than what you believe the other party is doing wrong.

Assertive communication will improve your interactions by lowering tension burden and providing social reinforcement while experiencing tough times. A respectful yet assertive 'no' to other people's unreasonable demands would help you to stop overloading your calendar and encourage balance in your life.

An appreciation of assertive conversation will also help you cope more effectively with challenging families, acquaintances, and co-workers, growing conflict and tension. Ultimately, assertive communication empowers you to draw the necessary boundaries that will enable you to satisfy your needs in relationships without alienating others and without letting resentment and anger slip in. This allows you to get in partnerships with everything you need while encouraging your loved ones to get their needs fulfilled too. Although many people associate assertive communication with tension and confrontation, assertiveness does actually encourage people to be closer.

Assertive contact takes place after much effort. Many people mix the term assertiveness for aggressiveness, but assertiveness is actually the balance between aggressiveness and passivity on the middle ground. Aggressivity contributes to hurt feelings and broken relationships. Passivity leads to frustration and resentment, and inevitably sometimes even lashing out.

Improve Your Communication Style

Learning to speak assertively helps you to value the wishes and interests of all – including your own – and to establish partnership limits while at the same time helping others to feel respected. Such measures will help you develop a healthier style of communication (and, in the end, alleviate stress in your life).

1. Instead of being judgmental, use facts.

When you tell someone about a pattern you'd like to see improved, adhere to accurate explanations of what they've performed, instead of using negative labels or phrases that express assumptions. For example:

Situation: Your mate, who usually runs late, shows up for a lunch date 20 minutes late.

Inappropriate (aggressive) response: "You're too disrespectful! You're so late."

Assertive communication: "We were meant to meet at 11:30, but now it's 11:50."

Don't suppose you know what the motivations of the other party are, especially if you think they're hostile. Should not presume in this case that your buddy came intentionally late because they didn't want to come or that they appreciate their own time better than yours.

2. Honestly judge the effects of this behavior.

It is a valuable start to be honest about what you do not appreciate about someone's behavior without overdramatizing or criticizing. The same holds true when explaining their behavioral effects. Do not exaggerate, mark or judge; simply describe:

 inappropriate response: "Already lunch is lost."

Assertive communication: "So I am left with less time to spend at lunch because I have to go back to work by 1:00."

Body language and tone of voice matter in assertive communication. Let yours represent your trust: stand up straight, keep in contact with your eyes, and relax. Use a sound which is steady yet welcoming.

3. Use "I messages."

It comes off as a criticism or an insult when you start a sentence with "You ..." and puts people on the defensive. When you start with "I," the emphasis is more on how you feel and how their actions influence you. It also shows more ownership of your reactions and less accountability. This helps to minimize the other person's defensiveness, model the act of assuming responsibility, and move both of you towards positive change. For example:

You message: "You have to stop that!

"I Message: I'd appreciate it if you'd pause it."

Do not hesitate to listen and ask questions when you're in a conversation! It is crucial that we understand the point of view of the other party.

4. Having an overall look.

A great formula for you to look at the bigger picture: "When you [their behavior], I feel [your feelings]."

When Used with factual statements, rather than assumptions or marks, this approach offers a more rational, straightforward, non-attacking way to let people know how their behavior affects you. For example: "I feel assaulted when you scream."

5. Notice the behavior, feelings, and the results.

An even better way to look at the situation is to involve the results of their behaviors (again, put into factual terms), and looks like this: "When you [their behavior], then [their behavioral results], and I feel [how you feel]." For example: "When you are late at the dinner, I have to wait, and I feel irritated." Or, "When you allow the kids, they can do something I've already forbidden, some of my authority may be taken away. Try to think of a situation that makes both of you win. In the case of the partner who is often late, maybe a new meeting spot will allow them to stay on schedule. Or you should just opt to make reservations at periods where your life is more flexible, and your lateness isn't going to trigger you that much trouble.

Seek a Solution

If you recognize the viewpoint of the other person, and they accept yours, it is time to consider a remedy to the conflict — a remedy in which you will all live. Sometimes a clear and logical resolution pops up if both sides acknowledge the viewpoint of the other individual. In situations where the dispute was centered on a misunderstanding or a lack of perspective into the point of view of the other, a clear explanation will work well, and an accessible conversation can bring people together.

Sometimes, a little more effort is needed. In cases where there is a disagreement over an issue, and both people don't agree, you have a few alternatives: sometimes you can agree to disagree, sometimes you can find a solution or middle ground, and in other situations the person who feels more strongly about an issue may find their way, understanding that they will grant the next time. The important thing is to reach a place of understanding and try to work out things in a manner that respects everyone involved.

Know When It's Not Working

Because of the toll that an ongoing conflict can impose on a person, it is sometimes preferred to maintain some distance in the relationship or completely cut ties. In cases of abuse, simple conflict resolution techniques can only take you so far, and personal safety is needed.

On the other side, incorporating a few limits and respecting the weaknesses of the other individual in partnership will offer some stability while coping with complicated family members. Letting go can be a tremendous source of tension reduction in marriages that are unsupportive or marked by continuing conflict. Only you will know whether a partnership should be strengthened or can be let go.

3.6 What Is Passive-Aggressive Behavior?

Passive-aggressive actions are those including behaving passively, rather than overtly violently. Sometimes by procrastinating, displaying sullenness, or behaving stubbornly, passive-aggressive people show indifference to suggestions or demands from families and other individuals.

Examples

Passive-aggressive activity can manifest itself in different ways.

For instance, a person may constantly create reasons for avoiding other people as a means of communicating their hatred or frustration against certain people.

In situations where the passive-aggressive individual is upset, they may constantly say that they are not crazy or that they are all right – even though they appear to be enraged and not all right. They reject what they feel, and fail to be emotionally accessible, shut down all dialogue, and decline to address the problem.

A key feature of passive-aggressive actions is intentionally procrastinating. The passive-aggressive adult may drag their foot when faced with assignments that they do not want to perform or appointments that they do not want to hold. For starters, if they are required to finish a job at work, they would push it off at the absolute last second or even show it on late to spite the individual who delegated the assignment.

Causes

Passive-aggressive attitudes may have significant implications for people-to-people interactions in households, romances, and also at work. And why is this often damaging behavior and common? There are a few factors that may lead to passive-aggression prevalence.

• Upbringing: some say that passive-aggressive behavior may arise from being born in an atmosphere where overt emotional communication has been avoided or not permitted. Individuals can believe they can't communicate their true emotions more freely, and then they can find ways to manage their rage or disappointment indirectly.

• Situation: The situation often affects passive-aggressive behavior. When you're in a position where anger shows are not socially appropriate, such as in a company or family event, you might be more likely to react in a discreet way when someone makes you mad.

• Take the easier route: It's not always convenient to be assertive and emotionally free. When it's difficult or even scary to stand up for yourself, passive-aggression can look like a better way to deal with your emotions without having to look where the issue arises from.

How to Manage Passive-Aggressive Behavior

So how can you respond when confronted by a colleague, co-worker, or even a sexual partner who participates in passive violence on a daily basis?

The first move is to understand the indicators of this behavior. The symptoms of passive-aggression include sulking, backhanded praise, procrastination, avoidance, and the inability to speak.

If the other party continues to behave like this, seek to hold the frustration in order. Alternatively, give attention to the emotions of the other individual in a way that is non-judgmental and truthful. If you're coping with a kid who's obviously irritated about having to do chores: "You seem mad at me for telling you to clean your place." The truth is that the person would actually refute his or her frustration anyway. It's a good idea to step back at this stage and allow the individual some time to work through these feelings.

Recognizing Your Own Passive-Aggressive Behavior

Recognizing passive-aggressiveness in others is always easy, so what if you are the one participating in such forms of behavior? Attempt to take a step back and have an unbiased glance into your own behavior.

• Do you still feel yourself sulking when someone else's upset with you?

• Avoid people you get angry with?

• Would you ever stop talking to somebody while you're upset at them?

• Set off doing something as a way of punishing others?

• Do you sometimes use sarcasm to stop serious conversations?

When you believe your interactions are being affected by passive-aggressive behavior, there are actions you should take to improve how you respond to others.

• Boost self-confidence. Often passive-aggressive acts result from not getting a clear idea of whether you are angry or what you mean. Start paying attention to what's going when you respond to various individuals and specific circumstances.

• Take the opportunity to create adjustments. Recognizing your own habits is a positive first move towards progress, but it will require some time to adjust the attitudes and reactions.

• Practice self-expression. An essential move in eliminating passive-aggressive actions is to understand your thoughts and strive to communicate your feelings properly. Conflict is an unavoidable aspect of life, so being able to clearly express your emotions will contribute to stronger outcomes.

Improving relationship with mastering communication skills

Conflict is nearly unavoidable inside a partnership. Conflict is not a problem in itself; nevertheless, the manner it is treated will bind people together or break them apart. Bad communication abilities, conflict, and misunderstandings may be a cause of frustration and isolation or a springboard towards a closer friendship and a happy future.

3.7 Tips for Effective Communication

Every time you're grappling with confrontation, bear in mind these ideas on good negotiation strategies so you will achieve a more successful outcome. Here's how.

Stay Focused

Even when coping with new issues, it's easy to dig up previous apparently connected disagreements. It seems important to discuss all that troubles you at once and get everything thought about while you're still struggling with one issue. Unfortunately, this also clouds the situation, making it less difficult to achieve shared consensus and a solution to the current question, and making the entire conversation more challenging and often frustrating.

Attempt not to lift any previous hurts or other issues. Keep concentrated on the moment, the thoughts, consider each other, and come up with a plan. Practicing meditation on your awareness will help you grow to be more aware of all aspects of your life.

Listen Carefully

People sometimes believe they are listening, but when the other person is talking, they are just worrying about what they're going to do next. Seek to realize if you are in a conversation doing that the next time.

Effective communication moves in both directions. While it may be challenging, try listening really to what your companion is doing. Don't disrupt. Don't be defensive. Only listen to them and look back to what they think, so they feel you've listened. Then you will grasp them more, and they will listen to you more readily.

Try to See Their Point of View

We tend to get our point across and be understood in a confrontation. To bring the other one to see it our way, we think a ton from our point of view. This is normal, but it can backfire to give too much of an emphasis on our own need to be heard first of all. Unfortunately, if we all do this all the time, there's little emphasis on the point of view of the other party, and nobody feels heard.

Consider seeing the other hand, and then you can describe yours smarter. (If you're not 'getting it,' ask more questions until you do.) Others will be more likely to listen because they feel listened to.

Respond to Criticism With Empathy

It's quick to believe they're mistaken to get angry anytime someone comes at you with criticism. Although feedback is painful to receive, and sometimes distorted or influenced by the emotions of the other individual, it is necessary to listen to the distress of the other individual and react to their concerns with empathy. Check at what's real about what they're saying, too; this can be important knowledge for you.

Own What's Yours

Realize that taking responsibility is a power, not a vulnerability. Good communication involves acknowledging if you are mistaken. When you both share a blame in a dispute (which is generally the case), work out what is yours and accept it. It diffuses the problem, providing a strong precedent, and demonstrates maturity. nThis also often encourages the other individual to respond with kindness, taking you closer to shared awareness as well as a solution.

Look for Compromise

Instead of seeking to "win" the case, search at options that satisfy the needs of both of you. This emphasis is far more successful than one individual having what they want at the cost of the other, either by compromise or a new innovative approach, which gives you both what you want most. A healthy relationship means seeking a compromise that will please all sides.

Take a Time-Out

Tempers often get heated, and it's just too hard to start a conversation without it being a disagreement or a battle. =When you get too frustrated at yourself or your partner that you can't be positive, or show some harmful communication behaviors, it's appropriate to take a break from the conversation until you both cool down. It can include getting a stroll and relaxing down and return to the discussion after some time, "sleeping on it" so you can digest what you know a little bit better, or anything you believe is the right match for all of you, as long as you return to the discussion. Effective communication also requires understanding when to take a break.

Keep at It

Although often having a break from the conversation is a smart move, do get back to it. If each of you handle the problem with a positive mindset, shared understanding, and a desire to look from the other person's perspective, or at least pursue a compromise, you will make strides in the aim of a dispute settlement. Don't give up talking until it's time to give up on the relationship.

Ask For Help If You Need It

If either or both of you have difficulty being polite through confrontation, or whether you have attempted to settle tension with your spouse on your own and the problem just doesn't want to change, you might profit from a few therapy sessions. Couples counseling or family mediation may assist resolve altercations and provide strategies for potential dispute resolution. Although your companion doesn't want to participate, you will always appreciate riding alone.

1. Recall that the aim of good negotiation skills will be shared understanding and seeking a compromise that would satisfy all sides, not 'winning' the debate or 'being correct.'

2. In every case, this doesn't work, but often (if you have a disagreement in an intimate relationship), it helps to lock hands or remain physically close while you talk. This can remind you that you both care for each other and that you value each other in general.

3. Keep in mind that being respectful to the other party is crucial even though you do not like their behavior.

4. Here's a rundown of that dysfunctional methods of coping with confrontation. Do you do any of those things? If so, your weak interpersonal skills could cause extra stress in your life.

6. Apps like Happy Pair can also be used to enhance the relationship.

Ways To Let Go Of Insecurity In Your Relationship

Stop thinking it is all about you.

You may get an ego-centric mentality seeking boogeymen where they don't live. When your partner doesn't feel like heading out, don't presume that it's because of you because they may have had a very poor day at work and depleted their strength just as quickly.

Stop psycho-analyzing any phrase your companion uses so that you can understand the meaning behind their speech, body appearance, and stance. Obsessing over secret significances is a sure-fire way of missing the argument.

Don't berate your partner for being too silent or repeatedly ask, "What do you think? "With any communication pause. One trait of an insecure individual is an intense desire to fill any second of quiet with meaningless phrases. Take the hand of your partner, breathe in, breathe out and appreciate the quiet together. Who said you couldn't just love sharing time without a conversation with each other?

Stop psyching yourself out.

The feelings may be the greatest friend or biggest enemy of your relationship. The consistency of your emotions affects the strength of your relationship directly.

Have you ever found yourself thinking cynical thoughts like, "I think they're going to get tired of me soon," or, "How do they accept me? "Such reasoning has nothing to do with fact but more to do with paranoia. In other terms, this problem doesn't exist that you're obsessed with — you created it!

Whenever you feel insecure about your relationship, say to yourself, "The thing I'm concerned about occurs just in my mind. I have total leverage. "

Stop lugging around all that weight.

Have you ever experienced such a bad relationship that you'd love to wish it all away, and you never have to hear about it again? Come enter the party. You're going to be hard-pressed to meet a guy that doesn't have a bunch of baggage because the thing called love is an unexpected (and often rocky) journey.

A little weight is absolutely fine, so before entering into any new partnership, you need to lighten the load. Let go of some left-over hurtful emotions that might linger, and know that your current partnership is a fresh chance to put all the mess behind you.

Life's lovely thing: You can restart as many times as you can!

Stop seeing things in black and white.

How can you keep your calm when someone accuses you of something you know is not your fault? Survey says: You were protective.

Likewise, approaching your companion with a problem — whatever that can be apparent to you — will most definitely lead them to become protective. Generally, that leads to a knock-down, drag-out battle, which is the opposite of constructive as you're still too busy fighting to show that you're correct to settle the disagreement.

If you have a question, do not point your finger right away, but address your spouse with sensitivity and empathy. Be relaxed with the reality that none of you is totally "correct" or "wrong." Somewhere in the center lies the true answer.

Stop feeling paranoid over nothing.

Let's face it: We're all talking to the opposite sex. Just by becoming buddies with a boy and girl doesn't imply the story has anything suspicious to it.

Do not be tempted to snoop your partner's cell, Facebook, or email address. While this momentarily relax your fears when you see nothing wrong, it is also a habit that may easily become addictive, not to mention detrimental to trustworthy relationships when they figure out that Big Brother is monitoring.

Stop putting off uncomfortable conversations.

Although tension is painful in the short term for your partnership, it will create the intensity of your partnership in the long term.

Facing the problems without any doubt will allow you to move closer to your mate. Never trim down words for each other, and you're going to build trust so high that you can tell your partner everything you're aware of. I realize that vulnerability may sound like a hidden secret, but the fact is that most people struggle from the vulnerability of some way. In reality, a Glamor survey revealed that 54 percent of women between the ages of 18 and 40 are dissatisfied with their bodies, and 80 percent of women recorded feeling bad while looking in the mirror.

Give your guy the skinny on insecurity. Let him realize you're doing your utmost not to let it get the best of you, but fear can still win out. Inform him that some sliding unproductive critique is not a reflection about him, and he need not do anything. However, maybe if he's in on the secret, he might give you a brief squeeze of the hand to tell you he's on your side.

Yet they are not all bodily insecurities for which we have to cope with. We also have previous interactions and encounters that have influenced our self-image and intimacy fears. Tell your man how dysfunctional past relationship has influenced you, telling you myths about yourself, marriage, and relationships. He would most definitely be able to connect.

Stop being dependent on anyone but yourself.

It's nothing short of amazing to have someone to embrace, touch, cuddle, make love, and share your life with. Yet you need to learn to respect yourself before you march out into the sunset in pursuit of life.

Just like you shouldn't welcome a guest to your home when it's a disorganized mess, if it's in disarray, you shouldn't welcome a spouse into your existence! Take caution if you welcome anyone else into your inner-house.

When you let go of anxiety, you should anticipate the side effects of decreased depression and improved happiness in the relationship. Do you remember the moment when the nervous green dragon starts to crawl up? Whether it's when you're looking in the mirror, or when you're passing some stunning street woman with your man. This is usually the time we try our partner's reassurance by venting out our insecurities.

Instead of depending on our partner to inform us what we need to hear at this moment, we need to pursue reassurance within ourselves. Note, the only person you listen to is your own fear. What we expect our partner to know is just what we will be saying to ourselves. Tell yourself at this moment: you're amazing, you're lovable, you should have a good relationship — address any doubt you have for yourself, mark the lie, and then contribute to a more assertive way of thought.

My mom once told me that anytime she began thinking to herself in a disrespectful way, my dad would suggest, "Carefully, that's my wife, you're worrying about there." This made her chuckle, but it also reassured her that her husband didn't allow anybody to speak poorly about his wife — even his own wife! When I'm inclined to let my fear get the better of me, I seek to consider that too.

Just say, thank you.

One of the main anxiety struggles is to take our other significant one at his word. Mostly when he says, "I love you" or "you're so amazing," we get a fresh surge of anxiety instead of feeling reassured and cherished. "Will he actually love me?" the voice in our head would taunt us, "You aren't perfect," the voice would claim, "He's only saying that." The urge is to doubt the claims of our partner, yet this kind of action may be toxic to a stable romantic connection. When you distrust him or deny him each time your man gives you affection and support, he'll feel hurt and insufficient. Do a favor to yourself — and your guy — and unquestionably chose to embrace some validation and affection. If your heart fills with uncertainty rather than affection, just say "thank you" and "I value you too." The actual act of undoubtedly embracing acceptance will help to make things simpler in your heart.

Challenge yourself.

Although being good to yourself and careful with your fight with insecurity is necessary, a bit of hard love goes a long way too! Sometimes, but definitely not always, feelings of discomfort towards our personal image may simply be more of a pride issue than something else — and thinking of it that way may be beneficial.

For instance, I've found that it's important to analyze my emotions at times when I'm more dismissive of how I look or catch myself contrasting myself to another attractive person in the house. The fact is, I don't really feel that I'm unattractive or unlovable more often than not. On the opposite, an urge to feel as good or attractive as I consider this other person to feel is probably something that bothers me. And, as humbling as it might be to realize, that's plenty like arrogance. The positive news is that by recognizing places of personal growth — whether struggling with ego or modesty, or whatever plagues you might have — you may carry much more flexibility over kicking comparison and insecurity to the curb for good!

Seek help.

Separating the myths from the facts is not a straightforward issue. Understand where the insecurities come from and start off on your own with a positive way of thought. When you are dealing with feelings of anxiety, then consulting with a psychologist, religious advisor, or psychiatrist will help improve your emotional stability and the wellbeing of your relationships.

The bond between yourself and the other significant should not suffer from feelings of vulnerability. You will feel confident about yourself and about love by approaching feelings of fear with sincerity, compassion, and a little bit of strength.

Chapter 4: Tips for a long and healthy relationship

You need to identify how your behavioral patterns are damaging your relationships so you can take some steps to save your relationships. You need to take a break and look at things from a wider perspective to see both sides of the coin so both you and your partner can reach at mutual terms. This will give you and your partner a prosperous life and make you feel like you have your life under control.

4.1 Stop nagging

Remember to carry the waste out? I guess I was telling you to clean the bathroom? You agreed you would quit smoking!

Does it seem familiar? It ought to. A screenplay from a nagger is just as full of suspense as a love movie that features Jennifer Lopez. And nagging, like a crummy Hollywood rom-com, offers no pleasure. It is not only ineffective but also erodes affection.

You're not right; you're just angry.

Nagging isn't smart; it's an act of negative emotion, says counselor Robert Meyers, co-author of Make Your

Loved One Sober: Solutions to Nagging, Begging, and Intimidation, and an addictions expert. Although rage could be reasonable and carried out of genuine concern for your partner — may be your husband is not giving up on smoking or your girlfriend began drinking again — you should realize one thing: Nagging will not help.

"People are so upset because they do something bad on a regular basis — whether it's alcohol or drugs — and they don't believe they should avoid it, and they only raise the volume of harmful energy they're throwing against others," Meyers says. "We find in our study that's the very reverse to what ought to be achieved."

Accentuate the positive.

What's a more powerful method to improve human behavior? Positive reinforcement, says Meyers, who claims that non-confrontational support is a more effective tool for progress. And if you may choose to berate your partner for coming home late, do not. Step away,' Meyers suggests. Or call a mate, and ease your feelings. Then, when you're relaxed, and your partner is more open to a conversation, remind them how much you enjoyed those evenings when you used to share dinner and joke and chat together. Through promoting passion more than rage, you would have a greater chance of reaching the core of your significant other than tripping their hair-triggering fury.

'When you're finished with a sandwich, love, would you clean the crumbs off the counter, please? 'That is an invitation. That's just nagging—'Donot fail to brush up the crumbs! '—when the need is not fulfilled. Because though being referred to like you are a kid is irritating, what the nagged person does not realize is that these crumbs symbolize a lot of emotional weight.

"When the question is not being taken care of after a bit, the nagger starts to ask why? A mind starts to wonder: "He doesn't respect me. He is slow. So then they transform into 'I can't trust you,' or 'I can't believe you,' or 'You don't understand what I have to suggest".

Naggers should not make crumbs or grinds of coffee in the sink a symbol for the relationship, Pregulman says. It's not because your partner doesn't think about you; it might just be that he or she couldn't give a toss for crumbs or coffee grinds. Still, on the other side, those who are nagged may want to remember how their companion thinks when they neglect their feelings. See how simple it is to contemplate the thoughts of other individuals!

To the person being nagged: Just do it!

For those nagged, Newsflash: It takes two to tangle. When you're irritated because after a wash, your wife won't avoid bugging you about picking up your soaked towels, so here's a solution (and no less from an expert!): "Just do it," Pregulman says. "I think if just five minutes are going to take, so what is the point of battling and getting disharmony into the house? "Mmm. Even a slob would consider the reasoning tough to disagree with.

To the nagger: Let it go.

Pregulman has concrete suggestions for the nagger, likewise. Rather than rant and rave about placing their wet towels on the bathroom floor to your partner or girlfriend one more day, why not just pick up the towels and get on with the day? Is the inconvenience of another supercharged domestic unease regarding damp towels even worth its weight?

Have some fun, Mr. and Mrs. Bickerson!

When you and your partner are bickering and arguing more than having fun and joy in life, try something revolutionary and productive: have fun together. Forget crumbs, coffee grinds, wet sheets, bruised emotions, and hiding surreptitious cigarettes, and reconcile in a relationship as loving partners, rather than as testy roommates. During the leaner, less cuddly moments that partners encounter, it's an investment during pleasant feelings that can payback.

"Creating a constructive [emotion] bank is profoundly essential to partnerships," Pregulman says. "I make the comparison to a bank account where it is not going to hurt if you have a ton of money in the bank, taking out a dollar or two. But if you don't, throwing out a dollar can actually hurt. "

Accept people with their imperfections

One way to achieve a healthy and successful partnership is to truly appreciate your mate for who they are. Many couples, therefore, struggle to realize this reality because they are either too busy searching for perfection or too busy dwelling on the shortcomings of their mate.

If you are having the same problems in your partnership right now, don't stress. This book will help you work out different approaches to help you solve these issues.

Here are a few inspiring ideas for discovering how to embrace somebody for who they're in a relationship.

Treat your companion like a real human.

And not only as an entity that should be revered and owned. Accepting others for who they are doesn't involve accepting them like a trophy or an item to put before your peers.

Treat them as a person who deserves care and love. Respect them as an individual, and embrace them as an equal. Treat them the way you expect to be treated, and be happy in your life that you have someone like them.

Respect their beliefs and respect their views.

You don't have to hold the same views all the time and adhere to the same convictions. As unique individuals, you will have the ability to your own understanding of the environment around you and respond to it.

Accepting somebody like they imply accepting the reality that you would still differ with not just one issue but several issues – so that's all right.

Accept their flaws and accept their imperfections.

But beware: there's a huge gap between acknowledging the shortcomings of somebody and embracing the violent actions of somebody.

The former tells about how you recognize the physical and mental shortcomings of your significant others. For example, your partner might not be as artistic as you are, or when it comes to socializing, they don't always share your trust level. It can be improved over time.

The latter, on the other side, speaks about how someone may be physically and verbally violent to their significant other. Acceptance to such shortcomings implies allowing them to affect you, as you always believe they can improve. This arrangement is risky and poisonous and should not be accepted.

Do not push them to adjust, but assist them in making them stronger.

It's cruel to ask anyone else to alter the way they conduct their lives. Above all, we are just single people who pursue various directions and are motivated by specific values.

You have to accept those discrepancies as a partner. As soon as you realize that they're not affecting their choices and lives, so you just have to embrace them and respect them for who they are. We should grow up with maturity and appreciation and become a stronger individual in time.

Learn their tale and see their motives.

Occasionally, you cannot comprehend that they are doing what they are doing. There will also be choices that may be frustrating to you, so there are also times where you start challenging your own wellbeing just because they don't align with how you choose to handle something. So how are you handling it?

You will know where they come from and what has made them who they are. You have to recognize their background and appreciate the lessons they've experienced throughout their lives. Trust them not just because you respect them but because you trust them to do the right thing.

Never equate them to those from your experience.

Never equate them to the individuals you've known in the past and enjoyed. It is an absolute deal-breaker with many and is undoubtedly the most difficult and hurtful act you'll ever do to your partner.

Love them for who they are, and seek no more. Go forward from the past and welcome the individual into your life. If this is not likely, then you don't deserve their affection.

Loving them within, for who they are.

First, what makes you fall in love with them? It's not their physical presence, but it's what's inside them- their heart and mind, their temperament, their eyes, and the little details that make them different.

Love isn't blind. Nevertheless, it makes people realize what they have lacked in their lives: a rare and extraordinary spirit that can add true love and pleasure to their days.

Understand they're not determined by their history.

Whatever they have done in the past has little to do with your present, especially in relation to your partnership. People grow, and they are entitled to be forgiven for the errors they made and for the poor stuff they did years before.

A history can be part of who they are, but for that, you can't evaluate them. What you should do to allow them to know you love them for who they are today.

Be careful and encourage them to rise.

Maturity may make a big difference when it comes to having a partnership work, but there are people that do not have the same degree of maturity and knowledge, particularly if they have this age gap.

No matter how happy you think you are, the gap in maturity will often have a negative effect on the relationship. Your job, as an older and more seasoned person, is this: anticipate them. Be cautious and direct them to be the best person they are meant to be.

Embrace your achievements and prove it.

Be respectful of your partner for who they are how they have improved. Knowing their experience, their stories, and the challenges they have bravely encountered, applaud them on a well-performed job.

The greatest way to embrace someone in a relationship for who they are is to be positive with their successes and show the universe that you are proud of them.

Know, there's no other beautiful and nice gesture to display your affection for somebody but to tell them they're great in their own unique way.

The Power of Empathy

"Empathy really is the center of the bond," Carin Goldstein, a professional marriage and family therapist, said.

"The relationship would continue to face problems without it." That's because empathy calls for kindness. And couples can not build a connection, without empathy.

'[A] connection is like a cement: if there is no binding, then all falls apart.' Psychotherapist Cindy Sigal, AMFT, also emphasized the value of empathy for a successful marriage: 'Empathy fills the difference between two independent people of varying experiences, emotions, and perceptions.' In her book Ideal Love, Imperfect Marriages, she cited John Welwood's concept of affection: "a potent made of openness and warmth, which encourages us to make real contact, to take delight in and embrace, to be at full with ourselves, others, and life itself."

According to Sigal, without empathy, we can't make this real contact.

4.2 What is Empathy?

There are various interpretations of empathy, said Sigal, who teaches at Urban Harmony, which offers therapy in the Chicago region. She likes the delineation of Psychologist Paul Ekman, which distinguishes empathy into three types: logical, mental, and compassionate. Empathy is a powerful force which helps to maintain the social order and cooperation. It's the process that allows people to consider others and to connect. Empathy is an essential prerequisite to friendship, belonging, and confidence. That is also the feeling that makes turning a blind eye to others' pain challenging.

Empathic individuals perceive a variety of rewards in terms of satisfaction. Empathy also facilitates altruistic action, and it has been demonstrated that empathy-based compassion promotes teamwork and acceptance, enhances bonds, decreases violence and judgment, and also improves mental and physical wellbeing.

Interestingly, evidence indicates that happy individuals seem to be less conscious of other people's negative feelings while being more empathetic. Therefore, it is important to exercise empathy, irrespective of mood, in order to achieve greater satisfaction for oneself and others.

Practicing the main elements of empathy will help you appreciate your life more and connect with others.

"Cognitive insight is often called perspective-taking, too," Sigal said. It is anytime one might picture how someone feels, but they are not aware of their emotions.

She shared this example: the wife appears irritated, and the husband asks if she's OK. The woman is recounting her extra-long drive to work. "Cognitive empathy helps one to understand the emotions of someone else without experiencing them or losing sight of whose thoughts those are," Sigal said.

It is emotional empathy. When you really have the same or identical emotions as the other person, she said. For e.g., when your partner's happy, you feel more relaxed.

According to Sigal, it is likely to employ both cognitive and emotional empathy in detrimental ways (e.g., someone may employ cognitive empathy to be manipulative; someone who carries on the feelings of their spouse may become too stressed out to help them).

Compassionate empathy "is a combination of constructive cognitive and emotional empathy that encourages one to respond as necessary." A messy person with compassionate empathy, for example, may understand and sense how frustrating or distressing it is for their spouse to cope with their mess, so they adjust their behavior and pick up after themselves, she said.

In other terms, "compassionate empathy is more like a whole person's response: spirit, mind, and actions."

How to Enhance Empathy

First, to maximize empathy for your partner, it's necessary to discuss "what's getting in the way of their natural expression," Sigal said. a"What are the situations where a person finds that they are behaving in a less empathetic fashion? "

Be mindful of your signals.

A significant barrier to feeling empathy for our spouses are being caught in our own experience and feeling pressure, Sigal said.

She recommended paying attention to what feels wrong about your body (to make you more upset) while you're struggling to handle your partner's viewpoint.

"For starters, is your heart beginning to beat faster, is your face flushed, or is your chest feeling tight? "When you sense no change in your body, pay mind to your feelings. "Are you going to get ideas shot out in rapid-fire, or are you always running the same thoughts in your head? "After finding the particular signals, take a rest. She said, "Take some long, deliberate breaths and wait until you settled down to rejoin the discussion.

Empathic affairs are a two-way highway. Enabling yourself to truly accept the feeling of another human will strengthen your interactions, and enabling yourself to be open to another will improve such bonds.

You provide ways for people to empathize with you by expressing feelings about your own stressful emotions, such as remorse, fear, and shame.

Being fragile provides two avenues to improve your own empathy. First, as it's mirrored back to you, knowing the importance of empathy will strengthen your dedication to being empathic towards others. In interactions with others, you often find greater confidence in handling difficult emotions.

Holding on to a dialogue about traumatic feelings isn't straightforward, but if you consciously learn this skill inside yourself by taking advantage of the moments that you have an emotion to express, you'll be better prepared for the receiving end.

Give your partner genuine attention.

When you listen with genuine interest, you take steps and consider your mate.

This also implies not dwelling on your own reaction or formulating a plan to protect yourself when they speak.

When you understand a person's feelings, empathy firmly places you in another person's shoes. Empathy doesn't mean like you'd feel in that situation; it's standing by yourself and spending a few moments embracing their feelings.

Many studies indicate that we excel in this role by mirror neurons or brain circuits that activate when we encounter the stimulation or see someone else experiencing it. Mirror neurons are responsible for beating the heart as you applaud competitors speeding around a crowd during your favorite athletic event or as you witness tragic blunders of pain.

When individuals are engulfed in the sorrow, disappointment, or anger of someone else, their sensitivity may not only stand next to them and comfort them with deeper compassion, but it also sends out a message that they're able to take on a difficult feeling so that others don't have to do it alone.

4.3 Practice loving-kindness.

Loving-kindness is the foundation for the activity of being conscious. It is clear of judgment and encourages peace and transparency.

"The deeper we are in contact with our base of adoring-kindness, the more we can reach empathy and be aware of our knowledge and actions. I suggest saying this affirmation of adoring-kindness: "May I be content, safe and pure.

May I feel passion, comfort, and intimacy.

May I be protected from hurt and free from terror.

May I be healthy, full of passion and laughter.

May I enjoy inner harmony and peacefulness.

May that love spreads to my life and all over the universe.

May (name of partner) be content, safe and full.

May (name of partner) has passion, comfort, and affection.

May (name of the partner) is safe from injury and free from terror.

May (name of the partner) is happy, engaged, and cheerful.

May (the name of the partner) appreciate the inner peace and comfort.

May love propagate across his life and the entire world. I also recommend doing the following loving-kindness meditation taught by mediation teacher and best-selling author Sharon Salzberg of the New York Times:"

Seek out the positive.

Partners sometimes get used to worrying about what's wrong with their spouse (or their life in general). That can rip you off empathy. Alternatively, try to look every day for a positive attribute in your partner.

Be self-compassionate.

When we can't sympathize with ourselves, it's impossible to sympathize with someone. I also emphasize the value of self-compassion, which is to "treat oneself with love, consideration, and empathy." Practice that by remembering and recognizing when you're having a bad time — without dismissing or creating a catastrophe the situation. Check-in then to see what you like about yourself. Keeping a list of safe approaches that you may turn to is beneficial.

Note also, that conflict and imperfection was part of being human. "It's not an indication that [you are] less than perfect, but instead something that is part of our common emotional nature."

Take Action and Offer Help

If empathy depends on engaging in unpleasant feelings, joy will decline. If individuals express extreme sorrow for the victims of a natural tragedy, they are moving closer to having themselves in the shoes of others.

Yet only experiencing the suffering of someone else, though it may enhance a sense of identity and being heard when shared, does not optimize the ability to boost well-being. Recognizing what another person is going through is getting the benefit that you can help understand what other people need.

Because empathy implies you're accepting the feeling but not the difficult condition that brought birth to it, you're typically in a more motivated position to support.

In order for empathy to be more successful and to optimize well-being, it is necessary to both sense another's suffering and also realize that you are in a position to do something about it.

In a classic research where participants observed another individual experience electrical shocks and were offered the option to support the victim by receiving the leftover shocks themselves, people who were strong in empathy were more willing to jump in to intervene even though they might easily switch away and no longer watch. Effective empathy helped participants to sense the discomfort of the shock they needed to help but not in a sense that they were reluctant to take it on themselves.

How to Accept Your Partner's Flaws

Also, in successful marriages, nearly 70% of disputes are ongoing ones that are never resolved. Sometimes at the root of such contradictions are attributes which one spouse has (or lacks) which annoy the other individual.

If it comes to enhancing the marital experience, it will also be beneficial to become more likely to recognize the qualities and shortcomings of your mate, rather than trying to seek to make them radically change.

Below are a few suggestions to be more appropriate.

Reevaluate the seriousness of your partner's flaws.

Often people become really upset with parts of their relationship, which are not even that big of an issue. It is quick to lose sight of this as anger builds up. For starters, I get upset at the problems of my wife with technology and being on schedule, but my annoyance is out of comparison with how critical both actually are in the grand scheme of existence. In reality, my partner is emotionally trustworthy and has several other positive attributes that are profoundly far more critical than our smart home devices being handled.

Acknowledge your own flaws.

What are the problematic attributes you have that your wife puts up with? It's convenient to see things from your own viewpoint in relationships. You can see all the things annoying you about your partner but think about all the minor ways in which you are a pain in the butt to deal with.

What are three daunting characteristics that your wife needs you to balance, but you're not involved in doing so? What are you indirectly (or explicitly) telling them to embrace involving you? For e.g., I'm quite fussy and controlling, and my spouse embraces these traits very well (more than most people would!).

Consider why particular flaws irk you so much.

When you're annoyed by one of the shortcomings in your partner, that may be mainly that you're reading something extra into it. For starters, I appreciate people holding their brains agile, so it is part of this for me to stay up-to-date with technologies.

I really appreciate having effective stress management strategies, but the fact is that my wife doesn't get as worn out from running late as I do.

Take a close look at the extra interpretations that you apply to your anger over the weaknesses of your partner. If you happen to be nervous, their deficiencies may cause anxiety for you. If you continue to feel uncomfortable about it (usually because of your past experiences), then their weaknesses can trigger those feelings. Seek to disentangle certain additional concepts from the interpersonal responses.

People who want to accept so much responsibility (which sometimes goes hand and hand with anxiety) are always disappointed because they cannot work out how to improve their relationship. It is one sort of extra sense that it would be helpful to let go of. It doesn't imply much about you if your spouse doesn't alter a little, irritating action, so don't make it about yourself.

Consider whether your partner should be required to value what you value.

I enjoy being tech-savvy and up to date with the technology, as described. I'm subscribing to weekly newsletters with information about how to use spreadsheets and found these abilities to be essential to life. Those are just my principles, however. There are not the universal ideals which everybody should have. When your companion is not driven to alter a behavior, it suggests some of their beliefs can vary from yours.

Look at your practical options.

When your relationship doesn't radically improve, then what are your choices, rather than constantly bashing your head against a brick wall? It will help you psychologically move on and learning about what the realistic choices are once you acknowledge your partner's shortcomings. How do you reduce the effect their flaws and deficiencies have on you? What precisely are the realistic workarounds? Since they always show the deficiency, how can you decrease the tension it causes for you?

For starters, the challenges in my life are fixed when it comes to time control if we intend to go somewhere 30 minutes until we really need to be there. When we intend to arrive 30 minutes early, we will finally be on schedule. It also annoys me slightly why that needs to be the answer since it's inconvenient and always involves waking up sooner than I might have wanted if I were only organizing myself, but the fact is that it eliminates the issue, avoids the most significant effects, and ensures we get to the airport on time, etc.

4.4 Understanding your partner

Travel together

When the Spring progresses, couples can schedule their summer holidays. In terms of your unique interactions and the wellbeing of your family, a couple of holidays can be a wonderful opportunity. According to a US study, people traveling together had better, happy marriages relative to those that do not. Couples in a happy relationship provided feedback that traveling together made them slightly more likely to be happy with their marriages, to connect well with their spouses, to experience more intimacy, to have a healthier sex life, to spend more time together, and to express shared interests and preferences.

Novel and exciting activities increase passion.

Relationships enable us to grow – to enhance our talents, our experiences, and our sense of who we are. So as they support us to achieve that, we become more comfortable with our partners.

When relationships are fresh, they are better able to help us develop ourselves. However, if we participate in self-expanding behaviors with our spouses, self-expansion will happen at any stage in a partnership.

A broad body of work shows that interacting with a spouse in thrilling and creative experiences enhances feelings of closeness and excitement. Field studies in which couples were required to spend time together doing something they all find enjoyable, and laboratory tests in which couples attempted fun, new experiences together, have shown that such behaviors improve feelings of love and closeness.

Travel provides numerous chances for fun and adventure, such as exploring new towns, going water-skiing, or seeking out a food you've never before eaten.

You may learn something about your partner.

One explanation why satisfaction with the partnership continues to diminish over time is because people seek novelty. Early on in a partnership, it's all fresh, and excitement is strong. Yet long-term partnerships also require soothing sameness. Through discovering different information about one another, we establish familiarity with others. It causes a gradual rise in trust during the early phases of married life. Yet even though you've been together for a long time, you will always know different stuff about your spouse, so this can be a perfect chance for a fresh encounter in a new environment.

A common goal and purpose

They have a common interest and ambition to see the future together. The excitement and yearning of unraveling locations, agreeing to an everlasting journey somehow binds these couples and provides them with a purpose to still want to stay together.

Understanding and adjusting to their limitations

Traveling is insightful not only to the outside world but to one another as well. We learn their strengths and vulnerabilities while we begin to explore routes and goals and figure out how to balance everyone on these tasks.

They have better communication

It has been pointed out, according to a study, that people who fly together cooperate more and have fewer conflicts than people that do not travel together. Traveling helps them appreciate each other better and making them better relaxed.

They have a better sexual relationship

partners that fly together have a stronger intimate partnership than people who do not travel together, according to a study. Traveling together reduces stress and depression in half, enough to ignite passion and excitement. More than three-quarters of those couples who traveled have confessed to having a healthy sex life, according to the study.

Experiencing something new together

The indelible riches graven into your hearts, and minds will be eternal as you witness everything together. What's fresh produces a history that would remain special to their relationships forever. Couples should view the holiday as a means to build good memories and significance in their relationships.

Remembering pleasant moments of a partner will enhance feelings of trust, as can reflect back on and chuckle at a humorous memory.

Couples understand each other well enough

When you're together much of the time, there's a little room to hide uncomfortable secrets. There are no facades, and the companion will be respected the way he or she is. Whether he snores, has un-shaved underarm hair, or has un-shaved thighs, traveling exposes a lot of uncomfortable facts. And there is nothing to avoid from this.

Their sense of humor is built together

You can't work around without a little fun showing up here and there. Often events can go terribly wrong, and you have to joke about it. It might be the terrible food that you just purchased in the street corner, getting your hotel space mixed up or missing a map. Something goes wrong, and it's enough to find plenty to chuckle about to hold that smile rolling all the way.

They live the romance.

It goes beyond what you see on the movie screens or read in every film, as a traveling pair you live the relationship out of spontaneity and a state of mind that you can be lead everywhere and something could sparkle another moment of beauty. It's never about the money but the interaction you might put together to travel. This is why in a poll of traveling partners, 86 percent of respondents claimed their partnership always had passion alive in it, relative to 73 percent of respondents who never traveled together.

They live in the moment.

Whereas other couples who do not travel together are concerned about the future and are constructing their partnership with uncertainties, couples who traveled together were not concerned about what will come next as they were overwhelmed and absorbed by the warmth of the wonderful moments they met each other. Traveling together did not allow them the opportunity to over-analyze their circumstance and be harsh about several subjects, but helped them enjoy the moment.

They have become best friends.

It's because they have only one another to turn to and fewer distractions by other entities or people. They have been able to give themselves everything and become better friends. Despite struggles and disagreements, they will hold to each other and provide each other with the support they wanted.

They are educated together.

Travelling provides a learning experience. And how do you feel about people who you are studying a topic with? The learning process brings them together and presents them with the ability to share their information while they expose their minds and hearts to the universe around them.

They are more forgiving.

Traveling together offers chances for making mistakes and revealing flaws. However, all along the journey, there are difficulties, and couples who travel together recognize the need to easily forgive each other and move on.

Experiencing freedom together.

Couples who have done tours together in the past love freedom and liberty that comes with the experience of travel. They will take relief in this empathy in recognizing each other's solitude, dignity, and sense of presence. It adds a further positive dimension to their partnership development.

Traveling together excites you and presents you with amazing opportunities to always stay alive.

4.5 Shared hobbies

Quite frequently, couples experience happiness, spiritual betterment, and pleasure at the start of a partnership. In other terms, they have a form of euphoria, which is not always a clear reason. You just love each other, and that relationship never appears to die. You still don't see the flaws in each other, because even though you run across them, they aren't a concern for you. The flaws of your spouse sound really appealing, and you may even value your spouse for possessing them even more. In this situation, with all its pros and cons, you love the guy.

Unfortunately, any pair faces difficulties in their lives sooner or later. For example, at the beginning, when you encounter a single female, you're happy to only chat and learn more about her, but after all, with time, you may find that you have absolutely nothing in common. Having common hobbies and interests is crucial to the romantic partners. So, you should have plenty of ideas to pick up on fascinating hobbies, for cases when facing this issue. You can, of course, leave your current partner and find a woman online, but what if you are in love with your current partner, head over heels? How to find fun activities for couples when partners have nearly nothing in common?

Can a Joint Hobby Strengthen Relationships?

It's a long-known fact that love attracts opposites, and in a couple, this leads to people losing common themes for conversation and no longer knowing how to further develop relationships. But even if this situation did not catch you, happy couples should always strive to improve their relationships, in any case. The response to this dilemma seems to be very straightforward, and it's quite convenient to find some interesting stuff to do as a couple. Sadly, it's not that easy in practice because so many considerations will influence the needs of your spouse and yourself. For example, partners often express similar beliefs, ambitions, and goals in a stable partnership. That's more important than just a hobby, while diverse and specific couple experiences will significantly help you develop a stable relationship.

It is really difficult to find something that puts two loving hearts together so well as activities couples can do together at home. You will know more about him or her if you discuss those activities and preferences with your partner. For couples, free activities are useful for knowing the principles of your mate. Occasionally attempting to introduce the partner to your desires is perfect because they will become your common ones in this way. Therefore, you are telling your partner you want to share some time with him or her. Don't fear, if your tastes are completely different and you are categorically contrary to doing something your spouse likes, and vice versa, you will still come to something new for you both. First of all, couples will certainly search for suggestions for shared activities focused on what is already in each of their lists of interests.

So consider exposing your companion to your new activities and desires, and vice versa. Yeah, this phase can take a long time, since it is not that easy to identify mutual interests. Also, you should never rely on just pure desires. So while you're trying to create or find a common purpose, you should also be searching for a couple's experiences and adventures. Even, you should seek to locate descriptions of interests that couples should do together.

So, how can the couple's interests improve the relationships? We have already addressed how your connection can be harmed by a lack of common interests and hobbies, but we have never stated how it can improve your life and partnership. As you may have learned, isolation is the biggest enemy of marital satisfaction, and the strongest methods to stop it are unique experiences for couples. Through doing something different with your friend, not only do you feel satisfied, but you also grow to trust your partner.

Ideas for Couples

Another terrible opponent of marriage is a lack of ideas for hobbies. You may understand the real meaning of common interests in partnerships, but if you don't have any clue regarding how to spend time with your partner, there's nothing you will be able to change. Do not criticize yourself if this has happened to your connection, but, as we said earlier, too many influences are impacting the effectiveness of romantic relations. It could be your partner for starters who don't really want to want to do anything you want. So, never dwell on problems, but pay attention to ways to solve them. Here we'll show examples of the top 5 couples interests that normally all partners enjoy one way or the other.

Computer games

A digital game industry encompasses nearly any aspect of human behavior, so anyone can find something that is important to them. You may, for example, immerse yourself in the Middle Age realms, war, magicians, and wonders picture yourself in the positions of architects, designers, leaders, or the military. Pick what you want and plan to plunge into the gaming environment.

Cooking

To each of us, it may appear to be a perfectly natural and normal practice, and we do it every day. Has cooking ever been one of the most enjoyable hobbies for couples? This has always been that way, in reality, but only if you can view this practice from the right angle. You should research multiple cuisines along with your partner, learn how to use completely non-standard items in one recipe, try something fresh for each of you each day. Remember that this is not about the results but about the process.

Photo shoots

It is a really complex activity. Additionally can divide the obligations. For starters, if one of you wants to be on photographs, while another tends to take photos, then it just works like clockwork. Currently, almost everybody has profiles on social networks. So you have several opportunities to post your hobby's results. Attempt to find various locations and clothing variations to make the photo shoots more interesting.

Tourism

Hundreds of couples think of going to other countries and towns. Traveling is usually a really enjoyable source of fresh feelings and experiences. And it's double as friendly and enjoyable to ride with your soul mate. Another advantage of this sport is that you should be able to stay active for several forms of travel, so everyone will consider something important to them.

4.6 Learning something new

When improving your skills, you will improve your partnership. This may be movements, international cultures, some musical devices, some activity. Select one that fits your needs. Often it's fun to spend time together enjoying various master classes, practicing new movements, languages, or even showing your friend how to play the guitar.

Since going through the phases of transition and growth, couples will not only find their partnership more complex and exciting but can also face conflicts and misunderstandings. In order to stay solid and consistent in your partnership, you need to focus on them. This condition typically annoys everyone, as it is not that fun to get the whole feeling that you ought to focus on connections. So what about love? All went very well and perfected after all. And, why does this wonderful and vibrant sensation, like a well-oiled engine, not work by itself? In favor of this allegory, we may claim this system has several smaller structures inside, and without human intervention, those structures won't work for a long time. In other terms, you ought to stick to certain laws to improve your partnerships and hold them at a high standard.

Know how to listen

It's really necessary to not persistently focus on the thoughts during any misunderstandings. Don't forget to listen to your partner's perspective. Romantic partnerships are not about demonstrating who's in control but developing a passion for your significant other. Consequently, all parties have the ability to vote. Don't let the feelings of your partner get away from you too, pay heed to what he or she has to suggest.

Determine what is important for your partner

Learning what's important to your spouse is crucial. Whatever you're grappling with, you still need to "hear" your partner as well as listen. Come to the realization of what matters to him or her and why. Typically speaking, this is the fundamental idea of satisfying your loved ones.

Respect

That's a pretty simple idea, but couples think about it very frequently. Know, love is the cornerstone of every good romantic connection. Once you value your partner, all quarrels and misunderstandings are simply a measure of courage, having passed which couples will easily progress to a new level, without dwelling on past disagreements and matters of shared understanding.

Be a team

Like we have already said, a romantic partnership is between two people who want to stay together happily. Yet becoming a pair includes always working as a unit and loving one another. For any given case, reciprocal cooperation is a symbol of a good and stable friendship. Also, if you disagree with your other half, don't openly show it in the sight of others, address this topic at home, and your companion will be thankful.

Watch your partner's body language

Sometimes you can face circumstances throughout your life where it is impossible to tell something and describe it to your spouse, too. It may be severe issues and mental misery related to the environment or just a poor mood. In either situation, it is really necessary to note shifts in the partner's attitude, whether they be in the correct or wrong way, reassure him or her that you have observed this, and want to improve.

The bond between two caring hearts in their perspective on life is often unique and different. And, beyond a doubt, each couple has it's own complexities and challenges, and each couple has a particular solution to fixing them. Then stop telling yourself, "What do people do on weekends?" and start considering the desires and preferences of your and your partner in seeking any matches. There is also one central concept that is ideal for all sorts of relationships: real love also demands that all parties strive tirelessly to strengthen their partnership. Only through knowing this definition will you create a healthy and long-lasting partnership that will offer you both pleasure and joy.

Accept Your Partner's Friends

You don't want those mates of your partner's. Maybe they're dirty drunks who try to drag your wife down their gloomy, drama-filled route. And maybe they're sexists who utter crass, demeaning things while you're around (things your husband is laughing off). You'd like to put a large X on the names of these men, but your partner is completely devoted to them and is protective if you hint that he should leave them. "You are not in a position to tell who I should be friends with," suggests your partner. And, "Together, we have a past." And, "You probably don't get it."

The alternative to this common marriage problem is, according to certain sources, a thing named. Acceptance. In the end, however bad you think about the friends of your partner, the truth remains that these junkies are a part of your life. Often you'll have to mingle with them (yes, including those that are more hideously irritating than chalkboard fingernails, including the two styles mentioned above). "At the end of the day, it's necessary to have a relationship at a certain level with friends of someone you want to be in a relationship with.

But friends of my partner really don't respect me. If you're not a mind reader, let's not say that's real. Let's rephrase that instead: You're not feeling relaxed with them — so that's more workable. "[Don't] encourage fear to be a reason for not wanting to communicate. You will not have to become BFFs all of a sudden. Simply propose to your partner that they allow to bridge the gap And seek to cultivate love. "Even if anyone is extremely irritating or disruptive, it's still from an insecure position. So seek to get past the scandalous conduct. Who knows what? Such people might just be socially unpleasant. Don't try to take it personally.

But They have a negative impact. According to Hartman, the first move in this case? Look at your companion well enough. Is she a drunken mess? Has he started being disrespectful? birds feathers don't all group together: As long as your mate remains true-blue, the course of least resistance is to keep quiet regarding his / her mates. "The last thing you can do is attempt to convince [your partner] to recognize his mates for what they are, which would cause him to run to their protection — and his own protection to appease them. This being said, you should convey your criticism of the actions of your parent's friends, and justify why you do so. So seek not to ignore these men at all. "You're asking your partner to select by failing to socialize.

But They're dumb. The key here is to treat the emotions in as non judgmental way as possible, since branding them fools is counterproductive. Undermining friends of a partner is undermining your partner. It's disrespectful and counter-productive. At some point, a safe, mature individual wants friends who encourage, help, and hold the same beliefs. "Calling 'idiots' friends of somebody's is a blatant criticism of the individual who has these friendships." Come from a curious location. .Get to consider what your companion loves in these friendships — it could even help you change your "idiot" viewpoint. I guess you can have a straightforward conversation without any judgments.

But They really don't want to understand me. It's hard not to take this seriously, particularly if you're introverted or come from an environment where you weren't 'seen' or respected. That's why it's worth debating the topic with your partner in this case. Write something like; I want you to make more effort to get your mates to understand me. You're expecting your partner to be open to your situation by saying it this way. You are learning how to integrate yourself, too. This makes the talk less, "Your friends seem jealous of me " and more "I want to be a part of your life." But all they do is discuss good old days when they're together. Frustrating! But keep in mind the creation of relationships of some nature requires time. You should definitely recommend to your partner that he/she should bring you into more recent life discussions so that you can engage. But you would have to make an attempt anyway. "Continue to facilitate discussions on common issues or social affairs — things that can be debated for anyone.

But I tried everything literally, but nothing seems to kick in. Okay, you have in common one great thing: You all have your partner in common. That must mean some form of mind-meeting, right? So if you've managed to be positive, communicative, caring, and accommodating, but you're still not getting back that attention, so take a breather. Display your help when doing something of your own. Talk to your partner like this: "Go out with your mates. Have a nice night! Please tell them I said hello."

Honesty is important in relationships

Honesty is important in stable marriages. It has the ability to create partnerships, to inspire, and to develop. What I think are seven explanations of why integrity is important in relationships, I'll share with you.

Let's begin with the first major reason. Honesty creates trust. If we are frank, we grow to trust each other. We don't have to worry about what's obscured or kept hidden. We are instinctively at peace in our nature since we realize that the other individual cares sufficiently to tell us the facts.

Honesty doesn't often sound comfortable at the moment, but we should respect it because the person being real is displaying vulnerability. They take a gamble to believe the honesty in you. Such people realize that what they might have to tell has the potential of destroying the relationship. They care for you, though, and want a truth-built relationship.

Based on reality, a partnership opens the door to progress. That takes me into the second explanation of why authenticity in partnerships is a huge deal.

Anyone who has a strong relationship is sure of this as being real. When we are in a partnership where two parties are able to be truthful, this offers the couple a chance to address problems that emerge. Misunderstandings do exist occasionally. If we are frank, we will move through the confusion, connect, fix, and cope with the issue. This may be difficult to have multiple viewpoints. Throughout our experience, however, we are both special and should understand how the other individual feels. Honesty expands the heart and mind.

In partnerships, the third justification of why honesty is necessary is that honesty develops our character. If we are frank, we keep people responsible for their actions. This inspires us and helps us to become a better humans. We become an individual who cares about our decisions, about how the relationship and the individual we care for may be strengthened or damaged by our actions.

Honesty helps people comprehend. This is so significant, as it can help us consider our experiences, present, and possibilities all around. When we offer authenticity, it doesn't automatically instantly reap comprehension. Yet when we've had enough people showing us the facts, it can be a perfect landing spot. From here, we will begin to grasp the circumstances, who we are, and what needs to change in order to expand any aspect of our lives.

Honesty teaches us liberty. Once we find ourselves in connections, we are able to be ourselves where we can be honest. We don't need to think about striving hard to be recognized or understood for who we are. It is talked about and exchanged, as we love. We don't have to wonder silently if the other person is irritated or upset because we realize they think enough for us to be frank about how they feel about us.

We learn through honesty. It imparts other wonderful lessons to us. It shows us how to communicate with people and carefully chose our terms. Think of it, when you recognize a little boy is saying something from an honest heart and it comes out as an offense. They don't try to be rude, not most of them, though.

They just speak the truth without worrying about whether their comments would affect the other.

The more sincerity we exercise, the better we know how to be truthful about our words, and use humility. We learn from situations in our lives what truthful words are successful in helping us evolve through great as well as unpleasant experiences.

Honesty is a representation of real affection. Happy and healthy households are aware of this fact. You want to shield people that you love from the evils of the universe. We don't exist in a world that is about sunshine and rainbows all the time. Some people (anyone who is reading this I believe can think of at least one, perhaps more) search for gratification at the detriment of another. Those who love most are super real, and the last thing they want for them is to see them hurt and weakened.

Spending quality time

Every single day, you see your partner. They're the first one you're talking to in the morning and the last one you're saying goodnight to.

But does a good relationship equate to seeing one another day in and out? Not really.

The easiest method of ensuring the relationship remains safe and solid is to invest more time with your partner. This includes spending time other than while watching Netflix or heading out for the occasional meal. Your relationship deserves more – and so does your partner!

What is the meaning of spending quality time? It involves sharing time without disruption with your partner. This is an occasion for you to come and speak together. Communication should develop the trust and emotional intimacy.

Quality time is also about the outward manifestation of affection. Not sex, obviously (though it's fun too!), just through holding hands, cuddling, caressing, and tickling. Research suggests such acts of intimacy will raise the happiness of your partner. And how will you spend meaningful time with your partner? Here are a few tips on how to make the best of your time with a partner.

Recognize the Signs

You have to know how to understand the signals that you need to devote more quality time together if you want a stable partnership.

These telltale indications include:

• All the time you are on your mobile.

• You prioritize spending time with your friends or other activities rather than spending time with your partner

• You aren't together at crucial times.

• You disagree more often or miss the link.

• You're not having reservations or date evenings.

• You don't feel satisfied.

Know that spending time together will undo the detrimental impact of the indicators above if you notice either of those relationship symptoms.

4.7 Try New Things Together

Do you ever decide to learn to play an instrument, or talk a foreign language? What about ballroom dancing or skydive?

Rather of treating these as individual habits and passions, why not have your partner involved?

Trying different experiences together promotes stable partnerships as it allows couples to rely on emotional and physical help on one another.

Shared interests also encourage marital cooperation, and the Journal of Happiness Studies reported marriage happiness twice as strong for people who treated each other as best friends.

Schedule in Tech-Free Time

The phone is a perfect place to listen to music, view videos, and stay communicating with family and friends. But is phone acting as a good thing for your relationship?

Many couples phone snub, or 'phub,' one another.' Studies suggest that phubbing will reduce the happiness of the relationships and raise one's likelihood of depression.

Reduce such chances by removing disruptions as you share time together on mutual bonding and making your partner feel like they have your full attention.

Hit the Gym as a Couple

One way you will invest more time together as a couple is to become partners in the gym. Statistics suggest that if you work together, partners would be more inclined to stick in their workout routine. Partners often perform more than they will individually. Another survey showed that 95 percent of partners who work together retained weight reduction relative to the 66 percent of individuals who did it alone. Enter a gym, perform st-home workouts for couples, pursue yoga for couples, hit the outdoor trails, or try cycling outside. Such physical practices will foster a healthier partnership, no matter what way you want to work out.

Cook Meals Together

Pop open a bottle of wine or bring some sexy music on when you're busy in the kitchen.

Cooking meals together is one of the strongest relationship strategies for sharing more time together when you both have busy schedules. Mix it up and attempt to cook a four-course dinner or a sophisticated French recipe together. It is not only an enjoyable way to pass your time together but also encourages coordination.

When all goes right, at home, you'll have a cozy date night dinner that you've cooked with your four hands. Even if the meal didn't work out the way you should have liked, you're sure to share a blast together and make fresh memories.

Have a Regular Date Night

Couples feel a stronger sense of satisfaction and less tension as they spend more time together. Having a date night in your weekly schedule is one of the main relationship strategies for a successful marriage.

The National Marriage Project has shown that getting a weekly date night will make your partnership seem more fun and can reduce disappointment in relationships. It also reduces the risk of divorce, boosts your sex life, and encourages good conversation.

Some interesting recommendations about what to do on your date night include: • Enjoy a movie marathon – have your favorite flicks together and cuddle up on the sofa.

• Play games together – Dice, board games, computer games, and other innovative opportunities are a good way to pass the quality time together.

• Replicate your first date – Return to the restaurant and order the same meal you had when you first met. You will spice up the evening by pretending to be there for the first time, meeting your partner and see how erotic the night gets.

• Schedule a weekend getaway – There's nothing better than going on a trip with the person that you love.

• Dinner and film-A treat!

• Find a new restaurant – consider rating all the Mexican restaurants / Irish pubs / Italian trattorias in your region.

• Have a lengthy love session – Intimacy facilitates the activation of the hormone oxytocin that is responsible for a multitude of wonderful emotions.

There are countless perks of having quality time together. Here are only a few of the aspects in which it will lead to a healthier relationship:

• Increases mental and physical affection

• Decreases divorce levels

• Enhances connectivity

• Decreases marital loneliness

• Stronger connections

• Increases partnership

• Enhances wellbeing

• Reduces depression

Which are all excellent excuses to start making the date night a daily part of the week.

If you set out devoted time to connect with your partner, it's easy to establish a balanced relationship. Do different activities together, consider your fitness partner to be your partner, and search for creative ways to feel near and attached.

4.8 Managing Anxiety and Conflict Avoidance in Relationships

Would convincing your partner that you don't want to go for the holidays to their families sound like it will turn into an intense drama? Will the thought of giving your loved one suggestions about how you want to be touched keep you awake with fear at night? Would you think that proposing an open partnership proposal would make your partner feel excluded enough that you don't bring it up and feel resentful afterward?

These can sound like isolated cases, but people view them as real issues in romantic relationships. Situations like this may sound like you're playing with a ticking clock, dismissing the sensation that gets you closer to an explosion. The combined impact left unaddressed by these emotions is like the detonating bomb, which can kill relationships.

A disagreement in its simplest form is a condition in which individuals have interests, expectations, or beliefs which do not align. It may occur whenever a decision is made or when conflicting needs emerge. It doesn't always end with a war or a debate. If we envision a confrontation with a partner, however, we picture disagreement, resistance, or negative feelings such as frustration, dissatisfaction, and disappointment. We are halting the discussion as a result. Often the difference between a dialogue and a confrontation may be vague because it appears to depend on the transition from becoming allies to adversaries.

The thought of resolving a confrontation, irrespective of the subject matter, always invokes terror and anxiety. People always believe that they know what their partner is going to suggest and perform in their minds whole discussions without allowing their partner a chance to weigh in. The assumption that you really know where the conversation will lead also contributes to denial.

The question occurs when individuals ignore problems instead of approaching them head-on. Conflict avoidance is a typical response to various interests that people don't interact explicitly with the problem. It is one of the main, if not the largest explanation why relationship issues exist. Such hesitation also happens when we are reluctant to communicate expectations, and we refuse to create requests. It could be that we don't think our partners to notify us without prejudice, or we're afraid they'll get upset and back off. Yet this urge to shield our partners from harmful emotions does not shield them, and actually operates against us, contributing to a lose-lose outcome.

An explanation of why people stop confrontation is bypassing the interpersonal effort involved in communicating their needs. However, the effort invested in resolving disputes is just as exhausting as articulating one's desires in the first place, or perhaps more challenging. Resistance in sharing feelings may often be interpreted as misleading or unethical. This erodes the confidence of partners and makes things much tougher for open dialogue.

So far, this has been a theoretical study of preventing confrontation. The only difficulty here is to bring it into action.

Like we discussed earlier, the fear resulting from the thought of thinking about something uncomfortable with your partner is like a ticking bomb. Think about a minor conflict as a relatively easy-to-diffuse firecracker, whereas a major dispute is something of an atomic bomb involving significant skills. A minor disagreement will serve as an opportunity to practice expressing the facts, such that when major challenges occur, the communication muscles will be powerful. Small disputes are also excellent testing ground for further learning how difficult circumstances are treated by both you and your partner. Actually, these are ways to obtain insight into your partner's responses and stay interested, so you don't create unreasonable conclusions.

The first step to progress in a confrontation is to accept the reality that you're preventing it. People sometimes don't notice the stuff they're ignoring because they're ignoring and instead center their energy elsewhere. One means of recognizing stuff you don't like is to note associative thoughts. Imagine those sensations are like the bomb ticking that points you in the direction of its position. Becoming irritable? Need to withdraw? Need to disconnect? Hold the thoughts and habits in mind, and you learn what to search for.

Here are several indications that you might be preventing a difficult discussion.

• You have something on your mind all the time, and it seems like there's rarely a reasonable moment to bring that up.

• You sound a little bit resentful.

• You are fearful of rejection by your partner(s).

• You feel detached.

• You are withdrawing from your partner(s).

• You feel as if you have not been treated well enough.

• You feel nervous about discussing an issue

• You are worried that your partner(s) may neglect you.

.• You are concerned that you might end up getting in trouble with your partner

It is necessary to brace yourself before you try to resolve a conflict bomb. You have to get in the best mood first. You want calmness, clear-headedness, and courage. In particular, bravery is crucial to start the daunting conversation, which involves leaning towards discomfort. Preparation may also include eliminating the daily mental shield. A ton of people go up with walls across life to secure themselves. It may appear as isolation or ignorance and can feel lonely internally. Removing the shield provides the potential for voicing wishes, expectations, and limits that might be terrifying but whose openness demands sincere interaction. Ultimately, it's important to understand that there's a risk that the explosion will go off, or your friend will scream at you, so nobody will die, unlike a real bomb. This may potentially, on the opposite, be an incentive for improved self-knowledge, development, and healing.

Being confused with what to reveal and when to communicate is always a barrier that may contribute to stopping confrontation. People are grappling over what terms to use as well as what can be more successful and what minimizes the possible damage to the other party. Instead of dwelling on managing the experience of the other individual, the better way is honest, open contact with your actual experience. For others, it could start with "I've got a story. "And" I'm concerned regarding. "It may even be something like" I sense a tightness in my heart "or" I'm afraid of losing you. Such thoughts are better handled as soon as you are conscious of them. The longer you sit, the more daunting the discussion is, and you may have fewer choices open.

And how can you really defuse a conflict bomb? And here's the measure.

1. Remember and recognize impulses (Identify bomb ticking)

 2. Locate sentiment root (Follow the ticks)

3. Find your desires, and/or limits

4. Let them connect

5. Engage in joint problem solving (Diffuse the bomb)

Let's explore the situation where you don't want to go on holiday with your partner's kin. You decide to take the opportunity now to rest and heal from a long, exhausting week at work. You can picture it turning into an intense disaster if you think about sharing the conversation with your partner. You agree that you feel frustrated and have postponed the discussion. In the expectation that the problem will fix itself, you may also catch yourself fantasizing about the car not working or the flight getting canceled.

In this situation, the ticking of a bomb is your anxiety and delusion, which shows your assumption that expressing your intention would possibly contribute to tension. By recognizing how you sound and stopping this discussion, you have found the device.

The next phase is to identify the specific expectations or boundaries. You understand the ability to prioritize self-care, and you express that to your partner. Solving challenges is about finding different solutions. Alternatively, you might think of traveling the next year, spending the holiday independently, or moving to the town of the partner's family but living in a hotel rather than in their house. The key aspect is working with the aim of achieving a win-win result while realizing and tolerating that an optimal answer may not always exist.

We generally view disagreement as a complex dispute, but it may be as plain and normal as a difference of belief, want, or necessity. That does not automatically involve harm or loss. It only requires discussion. However, denial is what causes disputes to become damaging.

More frequently than not, uncertainty and anxiety are the engines for confrontation avoidance. To quit resisting and resolving the problem requires both knowledge of the fear and bravery. Not all diffuse attempts would be effective, but you reduce the risk of an accident by recognizing the fear and making a sincere effort to resolve the problem. While accidents may still occur sometimes, if you have the expertise and skills in place to cope successfully with confrontation, the relationship would be substantially healthier and more stable.

Stop Feeling Insecure in Your Relationships

Insecurity is an unconscious sense of being challenged and/or insufficient in any form. At one time or another, we've all felt this. So though it's very common to have feelings of self-doubt once in a while, persistent anxiety will hinder your life-long progress and can destroy your intimate relationships particularly. Chronic anxiety robs you of your wellbeing and keeps you from experiencing happy and genuine interaction with your partner. The acts that come from insecurity — always asking for reassurance, envy, suspicion, and snooping — erode trust, are not appealing, and can push away a partner.

Although many people want to assume that insecurity arises from everything that their spouse has said or done, the fact is that most insecurity emerges from inside. The feeling may start with an unstable connection to your parents early in life or may grow after being harmed or discarded by someone you care for. Insecurities are sustained and founded upon when you equate yourself directly to other individuals and evaluate yourself negatively by critical internal dialogue. Most of the uncertainty in relationships is focused on unrealistic feelings and fears — that you're not good enough, you're not going to be happy without a partner, you're never going to meet someone nice, you're not really lovable.

When you begin to experience the sinking sensation of insecurity, there are a few strategies that you should try:

Take stock of your value

 when you feel vulnerable, you are always centered on something that you really miss. Each partner brings different qualities and strengths in the most well-matched relationships which complement the other. There are various forms of being equal. To feel more comfortable in a relationship, it allows the other individual to realize what you have to bring to the relationship. You don't have to be rich or beautiful to offer something — characteristics of personality are far more important to the overall quality of a relationship. Think of your personal traits — you can be sweet, trustworthy, humorous, caring, or a strong communicator. Many people admire certain characteristics in a partner. And think about how you make things easier for the other person: Do you make them feel valued, encouraged, and happy? There are aspects that everybody needs to feel in a relationship, but frequently many don't. Reflect on what you are doing more than what you believe you are lacking; it will shift your outlook. If the other individual doesn't understand what you've got to bring to the table, then that's their loss.

Build your self-esteem

Evidence reveals that individuals with greater anxiety in partnerships appear to have lower self-esteem. If you're not feeling confident about who you are internally, it's normal to want to search for affirmation outside of yourself. However, Trying to feel comfortable by gaining your partner's appreciation is a failing condition for every partnership. You offer up all of your strength while your life relies on someone else. A stable partner will not want to bear that kind of pressure as it can drive him away. Feeling confident about who you are in the relationship is a win-win. You get to experience the sense of well-being that comes with genuine self-liking, and self-confidence is an attractive quality that makes your partner want to be connected to you.

Creating your self-esteem is not as hard as it may feel. Creating self-confidence grows with maturity, so you can take two measures that can instantly change the way you feel about yourself. Choose to quiet your inner critic and cultivate self-compassion, and retrain yourself to concentrate on the things you want, rather than the ones you don't like.

Keep your independence

Two stable individuals shape a successful relationship. Getting too entangled in a relationship will contribute to weak boundaries and a fuzzy understanding of your own needs. Holding your sense of self-identity and taking care of your own wellbeing needs are the keys to sustaining a good equilibrium in a relationship. You feel more comfortable in your life because you're not relying on your relationship to meet all of your needs. Being an ambitious person who has plenty going on beyond the relationship always makes you a more desirable companion. Making time for your own mates, passions, and activities, retaining financial freedom, and setting expectations of self-improvement that are different from your partnership objectives provide opportunities to preserve your individuality.

Trust in yourself

Feeling safe in a partnership is based on trusting the other partner but, most significantly, learning to trust yourself. Trust yourself and realize that whatever the other person does, you'll be taking control of yourself. Trust yourself and realize that when it tells you something isn't right, you won't neglect your inner conscience. Trust yourself not to mask your emotions, trust yourself to guarantee that your desires are fulfilled and trust yourself, so your sense of self-identity should not be compromised. Trust yourself to realize that if the relationship doesn't succeed, you can quit and still be a completely functional human.

When you believe yourself, it is almost a certainty to feel safe. When achieving this sort of self-confidence sounds really challenging on your own, you may want to consult with a therapist who will help you understand how to do that.

It's necessary to note that no one is perfect — we're just bringing some junk along. But to be in a stable, safe, and successful relationship need not be flawless. You can not stop being a happier, more confident version of yourself unless you take your mind off on what other people say and hold the emphasis on yourself.

Conclusion:

As we look around today, our world is full of wars. Countries are breaking up themselves. One year, partnerships form, and the next break apart. The land's senseless bloodshed reddens. Refugees, finding a safe haven, dash from one frontier to the next. What are we worthy of doing?

Self Esteem has been lost amongst nations or collaborators, and kindness has gone missing. It's not meant to stay that. People will move into relationships. Knowing the solutions to old destructive methods is also what they need. They sometimes require further change, healing, and resurrection still. Fundamentally, they pose a decision at any stage. Are we choosing to love or to hate here? To pull forward or to strike and approach?

All the couples have to do is to set out their options and observe from the sidelines. It's an expression of what's best about them, the potential to learn, have compassion, and love again if they make the decision to love.

CPSIA information can be obtained
at www.ICGtesting.com
Printed in the USA
BVHW042328140221
599917BV00021B/100